Psalms of Solomon
A New Translation and Introduction

Apocrypha and Pseudepigrapha Texts
NUMBER 1

Psalms of Solomon

A New Translation and Introduction

Heerak Christian Kim

The Hermit Kingdom Press
Highland Park * Seoul * Bangalore * Cebu

Psalms of Solomon: A New Translation and Introduction
(Apocrypha and Pseudepigrapha Texts, 1)

Copyright ©2008 Heerak Christian Kim

All rights reserved. No part of this book may be reproduced in any form or by any means, electronic or mechanical, including photocopying, recording, or by any information storage and retrieval system (including computer files in any form), without permission in writing from the publisher.

Hardcover ISBN13: 978-1-59689-079-4
Paperback ISBN13: 978-1-59689-080-0

Write To Address:
The Hermit Kingdom Press
P. O. Box 1226
Highland Park, NJ 08904-1226
The United States of America

Library of Congress Cataloging-in-Publication Data

Psalms of Solomon. English.
 Psalms of Solomon : a new translation and introduction / Heerak Christian Kim.
   p. cm. -- (Apocrypha and pseudepigrapha texts ; no. 1)
 Includes bibliographical references and index.
 ISBN 978-1-59689-079-4 (hardcover : alk. paper) -- ISBN 978-1-59689-080-0 (pbk. : alk. paper)
 1. Psalms of Solomon--Introductions. I. Kim, H. C. (Heerak Christian) II. Title.
 BS1830.P7A3 2008
 229'.912--dc22
                    2008021148

Dedicated to Professor Jody Pinault of Santa Clara University, who was my first instructor of Classical Greek at the University of Pennsylvania, during my undergraduate years (1987-1990). It was she who put me on the road of love for the classical Greek language and ancient Greek texts.

Table of Contents

Preface   iii

"Psalms of Solomon" Text   1

Chapter One   23
   "The Psalms of Solomon in the Context of
   Second Temple Jewish History"

Chapter Two   42
   "The Psalms of Solomon in the Context of Late
   Second Temple Period Jewish Denominations"

Chapter Three   60
   "The Psalms of Solomon as a Quintessential
   Late Second Temple Document"

Chapter Four   85
   "The Covenant"

Bibliography   103

Index   109

Psalms of Solomon

Preface

In private conversation, Professor William Horbury, the resident Jewish Studies expert at Cambridge University mentioned that most of the ancient Jewish literature would have been lost if it were not for Christians, who transmitted the text through manuscript copies, edited texts, translations, and commentaries. Of course, this is common knowledge in the academic world and Professor Marinus de Jonge, the Jewish Studies expert at Holland's world-famous Leiden University has, for many years, emphasized this fact in his lectures and publications. Credit is due, where it is due, and history should be remembered.

One of the reasons why this historical fact is overlooked is due to ignorance. Many people suppose that Jews preserved Jewish texts. This is true of the Talmud, which is the sacred religious text of Rabbinic Judaism. And this is true, in some part, to the Old Testament, which many Jewish scholars refer to as "Hebrew Scriptures" due to their discomfort with Christianity and its appellation of it as the first part of its canon. But even with the Old Testament, greatest textual studies have always been done by Christian theologians and clergy, and not Jewish rabbis of Rabbinic Judaism. In fact, the authoritative Old Testament text in Hebrew for scholarly research (*Biblia Hebraica Stuttgartensia* edition) is produced by Christians – to be specific, the German Bible Society, in Stuttgart, which also happens to be the home-base of BMW automobile company, which has produced automobiles for Germany and the world since 1929 (and motorcycles since 1923). The Hebrew Bible text produced by leading Jewish publication societies and agencies is deemed inferior and not worthy of academic research

Preface

even by Jewish experts at leading Jewish institutions, such as Jewish Theological Seminary of America, Hebrew Union College, and the Hebrew University of Jerusalem in Israel.

Another reason for why the fact of Christian contribution to the preservation of Jewish texts for over 2000 years is denigrated is that many Jews do not like the historical fact. Many Jews find it embarrassing. In fact, some of the greatest experts of Jewish studies and those who contributed greatest to the learning of Hebrew texts were unapologetic Nazis in Germany who called for the annihilation of the Jews. For some Jewish experts of the Old Testament, they feel awkward about using research, however valuable to scholarship, done by those who participated in the extermination of Jews in Germany and Poland, but they realize that they cannot get anywhere in academia without using their research. So, they pretend ignorance or downplay the historical reality.

But the question is not as irrelevant as one might think. In a doctoral seminar at Brown University, taught by Professor Stan Stowers, who is a Jewish Studies expert, he raised the question, whether it was legitimate to use scholarship by Professor Mircea Eliade of the University of Chicago (1907-1986), when Prof. Eliade was an avid supporter of the Nazis during World War 2. The modern study of religion (particularly in secular universities) in the United States of America is impossible without Prof. Eliade. Basically the question was: Should scholarship from anti-Semites be discarded in researching into Jewish Studies? The doctoral seminars divided emotionally into those who said "no" (mixture of Jews and non-Jews) and those who said "yes" (all Jews). But of course, the discussion was a mute exercise, because one cannot ignore Prof. Eliade and call herself an expert of religion, at least in the United States of America. But an important argument in support of using his research was the point that ancient history is just that – ancient history. A person in the modern world is equally biased or objective as the next person when it comes to the ancient world. However, one comment was raised that Jews may be more biased when it comes to the past because of current invested Jewish interests in Israel and the Arab-Jewish conflict. Although the Brown discussion was a how-many-angels-can-dance-on-the-top-of-a-nail discussion in many ways, it cannot be denied that for some, especially Jewish academics concerned with Jewish communal interests of the present and identity questions which they project into the past, it is a relevant question. Should research of "anti-Semities" (however defined?) be used in academic research?

Especially given the fact that Jewish Studies in America has developed along polemic lines against Christianity, experts of Jewish Studies in the United States of America are often dedicated to active or passive whitewashing of Christian contributions to Jewish Studies, or the Christian leadership of Jewish Studies, which has been the case by-in-large for over 2000 years in the scholarly world. Even now, the leading experts of Jewish Studies are mostly Christians and Christian clergy in the United States (such as Professor John Collins of Yale University Divinity School and James Charlesworth of Princeton Theological Seminary) and in other parts of the world (such as Professor William Horbury in Great Britain and Professor Marinus de Jonge in continental Europe).

In the end, it is understandable why the leading experts of Jewish Studies are Christians. Christianity has always investigated Judaism and Jewish history with a view to understanding it in the context of the history of Christianity. Hundreds of books in Barnes and Nobles and Borders bookstores testify to this fact. Christian scholars and clergy have always been interested in Jewish Studies. Secondly, it is a simple numbers game. There are just so many more Christians than Jews in the world that the best experts of Jewish Studies are bound to be Christians and not Jews. Thirdly, Christian communities are interested in maintaining excellence in Jewish Studies research, by endowing many professorships in the field. This is true for Christian denominational seminaries, like

Preface

Princeton Theological Seminary of the Presbyterians, Duke University Divinity School of the Methodists, and the Catholic University of America, as it is for non-denominational Christian seminaries, like Fuller Theological Seminary and Gordon-Conwell Theological Seminary, which produce Christian clergy as well as Christian academic scholars of Jewish Studies. And this will not change because there are over one billion Christians around the world and only about 12 million Jews around the world.

Although some Jews may find it disturbing that Christians will always carry the torch of Jewish Studies research, for the discipline of Jewish Studies, it is nice to know that excellence in Jewish Studies scholarship will be maintained precisely because there are numerous numbers of bright and dedicated Christians willing to devote their entire life to Jewish Studies scholarship. It has always been that way, and it will always be that way.

But Jews cannot testify that they hold monopoly in accurate interpretation in Jewish Studies. Since the founding of the Jewish Theological Seminary by Professor Solomon Schlechter, Jewish seminaries in America have been dedicated ideologically to Zionism and Jewish identity discourse. Their scholarship into ancient Jewish history has been colored by these agenda, as recognized even by leading Jewish Studies experts, who are religiously Jews and leaders of Jewish communities. Some even print in their college Jewish Studies program brochures that their program is meant to uphold the Jewish community. This may be a ploy to get funding from wealthy Jewish businessmen, but this does not belie the reality of the situation in America and elsewhere.

Furthermore, Judaism around the world today is Rabbinic Judaism, dependent on the Talmud, which was written down over 500 years after the birth of Jesus of Nazareth in Palestine. Rabbinic Judaism of today is nothing like the Temple worship of Jews during the time of Jesus. It is arguable that they are two completely different religions; one involves sacrifice and propitiation, the other involves legal dedication. In fact, many in Jewish religious circles have used the term Early Judaism to refer to the Late Second Temple Period because they believe that it is there when the seeds of Rabbinic Judaism were planted. Of course, these Jewish experts presume the difference between the sacrifice-based religion of the Temple Period and the Talmud-law based Rabbinic Judaism, which is the "Judaism" of today. There is no Temple-based Judaism today because the Temple mount in Jerusalem is currently occupied by a Muslim mosque and Muslim worship is conduced every week there. And most leaders of Rabbinic Judaism are not interested in Temple-based worship because a revival of such a religion would totally disenfranchise them and their leadership. In fact, a successful revival of Temple worship in Jerusalem will mean the end to Rabbinic dominance in the Jewish world. Most leaders of Rabbinic Judaism (whether they are orthodox, conservative, or reformed) are not interested in such a reality.

The Psalms of Solomon is an important document from the ancient world that describes a different reality than that which Jews around the world find themselves, today. Rabbinic Judaism or proto-Rabbinic Judaism was negligible. Some experts number members of the Pharisees at the time of Jesus to tens of thousands and not much more. While the Jerusalem Temple stood, they just could not gain complete ascendancy. The Psalms of Solomon was written at a time in which it was a given that religious authority resided in the Jerusalem Temple and its legitimate priests. The question was not whether the *auctoritas* resided with the Jerusalem Temple and its priests, but whether the right priests were in positions of power. In other words, the permutation of religious authority around the Jerusalem Temple was not questioned, and the fact of priestly authority over the Jewish populace was not doubted. The question was: Were the right priests occupying the Jerusalem Temple and its leadership.

The Psalms of Solomon is an important Jewish text from the Late Second Temple period, which highlights this reality. In

Preface

fact, as a document written by a Zadokite priest in support of Zadokite priests who have been displaced from Jerusalem Temple authority positions, he illustrates through couched language why the Zadokites were the legitimate priests who should be in the Jerusalem Temple and occupy its leadership. Writing at a time when the Hasmonean coup-de-tat was complete and the Hasmoneans have secured their power at the Jerusalem Temple and over the population in Jerusalem, the Zadokite author could not write as blatantly for fear of his life. But the precarious historical situation has given us in the 21st century a document of exquisite worth. The Psalms of Solomon is quintessentially "Jewish" in terms of its support of the Jerusalem Temple and priestly authority. However, it is a propaganda tract par excellence in support of the displaced Zadokite priests.

In light of the Dead Sea Scrolls and its historical-evidential convergence with the ideas of the Psalms of Solomon, it cannot be denied that the Psalms of Solomon holds at least one key to unlocking the reality of the ancient world in Palestine during the time of the Hellenistic Era, or the Late Second Temple Period. The Psalms of Solomon, written during the Hellenistic Period, was written in Greek.

Psalms of Solomon

PSALM 1

A Psalm of Solomon.

¹I cried out to the LORD when they afflicted me continually – to God when the sinners attacked. ²Suddenly, the sound of war resounded before me. Let him hear me, because I am full of righteousness! ³I reasoned in my heart that I was filled with righteousness because I was fruitful and had many children. ⁴Their wealth extended over all the earth and their glory to the end of the earth. ⁵They were raised to the stars. They said that they would never fall. ⁶But they grew proud in their good situation and they could not contain it. ⁷Their sins were in secret, so I did not know. ⁸Their sins were over the people before them; ⁹they completely defiled the holiness of the LORD.

Heerak Christian Kim

PSALM 2
A Psalm of Solomon about Jerusalem.

¹When the sinner became haughty, he rammed through the surrounding wall with a battering ram, and you did not stop it. ²Strange peoples went up to your altar, stomping with their sandals in pride, ³because the sons of Jerusalem desecrated the holiness of the LORD and defiled the gifts of God with transgressions. ⁴On account of these things, He said, "Expel them far from me." He did not prosper them. ⁵The beauty of his glory – it was made into nothing before God; it was totally dishonored. ⁶The sons and the daughters were in horrible captivity – their neck stamped, branded among the peoples. ⁷He treated them according to their sins; for, he relinquished them into the hands of the oppressors. ⁸He moved his countenance away from being merciful to them – the young and the old and their children together. ⁹For, they did evil together, not listening. ¹⁰And the heaven lamented, and the earth hated them, ¹¹because no man had done all the things on it in the manner that they had done. ¹²And the earth will know all your righteous judgment, O God. ¹³God set the sons of Jerusalem in derision before prostitutes in it; everyone who passed by went in before the sun. They mocked with their transgressions. ¹⁴Just as they were doing, they showed off their injustices before the sun. And the daughters of Jerusalem were defiled according to your judgment, ¹⁵because they desecrated themselves in the confusion of intercourse. My stomach and my feelings are in pain regarding these. ¹⁶I will justify you, O God, in the uprightness of heart, because in your judgments is your righteousness, O God; ¹⁷for, you repaid the sinners according to their works, according to their sins, which were very evil. ¹⁸You revealed their sins, so that your judgment might ap-

Psalms of Solomon

pear. [19]You annihilated their memory from the earth. God is a righteous judge and will not marvel at a face. [20]He thrust down her beauty from the throne of glory; for, the Gentiles denigrated Jerusalem in trampling underfoot. [21]She put on sackcloth instead of a beautiful garment, a rope around her head instead of a crown. [22]She put off the diadem of glory, which God had placed on her. [23]Her beauty was thrust down on the earth in dishonor. [24]And I saw and beseeched the face of the LORD and said, "Enough, O LORD! May your hand not be heavy upon Israel in bringing the Gentiles." [25]For, they jeered and did not spare in wrath and anger with vengeance, [26]and they would have been brought to an end completely, if you, O LORD, had not punished them in your wrath. [27]For, they have done not in zeal, but in the lust of the heart, [28]to pour out their anger against us in endlessness. Do not delay, O God, to repay them in their heads, [29]so that they might speak about the pride of the dragon in dishonor. [30]And it was not long until God showed to me that proud one, pierced on the mountains of Egypt, made less than the least on earth and the sea. [31]His body was destroyed on the waves in much pride, and there was not one who would bury, [32]because he rejected him in dishonor. He did not consider that he was a man, and he did not consider the end. [33]He said, "I will be the lord of earth and sea." And he did not perceive that God is great, mighty in his power and greatness. [34]He is king over the heavens, and he judges kings and rulers. [35]He raises me into glory, and he denigrates the proud into eternal damnation in dishonor, because they did not know him. [36]And now see, people of high status on earth, the judgment of God! For, he is a great and righteous king, who judges over the heaven. [37]Praise God, those who fear the LORD with understanding! For, the mercy of the LORD is on those who fear him, with judgment ³⁸to discriminate between the righteous and the sinner, to destroy the sinners for eternity according to their works, ³⁹to show mercy to the righteous one from the oppression of the sinner, and to destroy the sinner for what he has done to the righteous. ⁴⁰For, the LORD is gracious to those who call upon him in patience, to do according to his mercy to those with him, to stand through all time before him in power. ⁴¹May the LORD be praised into the eternity in front of his slaves!

PSALM 3
A Psalm of Solomon about the Righteous.

¹O soul, why do you sleep and not praise the LORD? ²Sing a new song to God who is worthy! Sing and be awake to his being awake; for, it is good to praise God with the whole heart. ³The righteous remember the LORD with praising through everything and declare as righteous the judgments of the LORD with thanksgiving. ⁴A righteous man does not despise being chastised by the LORD; his pleasure is always for the LORD. ⁵The righteous man encounters a barrier and declares the LORD as righteous; he falls into misfortune and looks for what the LORD will do for him. ⁶He observes where his salvation will come from. ⁷The truth for the righteous is from God their Savior. Sin upon sin does not lodge in the house of the righteous. ⁸The righteous man searches his house all the time to push away unrighteousness. With his sin offering, ⁹he atones for his sins committed unknowingly, and with fasting, he afflicts his soul. ¹⁰And the LORD purifies every holy man and his house. ¹¹A sinful man encounters a barrier and curses his life, the day of his birth, and the birth pangs of the mother. ¹²He adds sin upon sin during his life. ¹³He

falls into misfortune because his body is evil, and he will not rise. The destruction of the sinner is forever. ¹⁴And the LORD will not remember him when he visits the righteous. ¹⁵This is the fate of the sinners into eternity. ¹⁶But those who fear the LORD will arise to everlasting life, and their life will be in the light of the LORD and will not fail anymore.

PSALM 4

A Psalm of Solomon against Men-Pleasers.

¹O defiled one, how do you sit in the assembly when your heart is far removed from the LORD? You provoke the God of Israel with your transgressions. ²He is excellent in words, excellent in his distinctive mark over all; he is austere in words when he condemns sinners in judgment. ³And his hand is at first against him as if in zeal, but he is himself guilty in variety of sins and in incontinence. ⁴His eyes are on every woman without distinction; his tongue is false when he makes a contract with an oath. ⁵At night and in secret, he sins as if he were not seen; with his eyes, he communicates with every woman in evil compact. ⁶He is quick to enter every house with a cheerful look as if he were not evil. ⁷May God destroy those who live in hypocrisy among the holy ones and destroy his life in the corruption of his flesh and in poverty! ⁸May God bring out into open the deed of the men who are men-pleasers and bring out into open his deed in derision and scorn! ⁹And may the holy ones declare righteous the judgment of their God as the sinners are destroyed before the face of the righteous one, ¹⁰and the men-pleaser uttering law with deceit is destroyed! ¹¹And their eyes are in the house of the man who is successful like a serpent, to corrupt wisdom, speak-

ing in the words of transgressors. ¹²His words are deceitful in order to accomplish his unrighteous desire. ¹³He did not stop until he succeeded to scatter as if in lamentation, and he made desolate because of his evil desire. ¹⁴He deceived with words, saying that there is no one who sees and judges. ¹⁵He was filled with transgression in this, and his eyes are on another's house to destroy with clamorous words. His soul is not satisfied in all this. ¹⁶O LORD, may his fate be dishonor before you; his exiting be in groans and his entering in a curse! ¹⁷O LORD, may his life be in pain, poverty, and difficulty; his sleep in pain and his awaking in difficulties! ¹⁸May sleep be taken away from his eyelids at night; may he fail from all the work of his hands in dishonor! ¹⁹May he enter his house empty in his hand, and may his house be in lack of all that which could satisfy his soul! ²⁰May his old age be in the solitude of childlessness until his being taken away! ²¹May the bodies of the men-pleasers be torn in pieces by beasts, and may the skeleton of the transgressor be in dishonor under the sun! ²²May ravens peck out the eyes of hypocritical men! ²³For, they have destroyed many men's houses in dishonor and scattered them in their lust. ²⁴They neither remembered God, nor feared God in all these things. ²⁵They both angered and offended God, by cutting them off from the earth, because they deceived the souls of the good with craftiness. ²⁶Blessed are those who fear the LORD in their goodness! ²⁷The LORD will deliver them from deceitful and sinful men and will deliver us from all the snares of the transgressing one. ²⁸May God destroy those who commit every injustice in pride, because our God, who is righteous, is a great judge and a mighty LORD. ²⁹O LORD, may your mercy be on all who love you!

Psalms of Solomon

PSALM 5
A Psalm of Solomon.

¹O LORD, who is God, I will praise your name with joy in the midst of those who know your righteous judgment. ²For, you are gracious and merciful, a refuge for the poor one. ³When I cry out to you, do not be silent to me. ⁴For, no one takes booty from a powerful man, ⁵and who will take from all which you have made, unless you give? ⁶For, the man and his fate, against you in computation, will not add to increase against your judgment, O God. ⁷In our plight, we will call out to you for help, and you will not reject our prayer, because you are our God. ⁸May your hand not be heavy upon us, so that we will not sin out of pure necessity for food. ⁹Even if you do not bring us back from captivity, we will not stay away, but come to you. ¹⁰For if I am hungry, I will cry out to you, O God, and you will give me. ¹¹You feed the birds and the fish; when you give rain to desert places making the grass grow, you give fodder to all living in the desert. ¹²And if they are hungry, they will lift their face to you. ¹³You feed kings and rulers and peoples, O God, and who is the hope of the poor and needy one, if not you, O LORD? ¹⁴And you will listen, because who is gracious and gentle but you? You gladden the heart of the humble one when you open your hand in mercy. ¹⁵This is the kindness of a man for his friend, today and tomorrow, if he repeats help without complaining, and you would be surprised at this. ¹⁶But your gift is great according to your kindness and extravagant, and he who is with you, O Lord, the Hope, he will not be lacking in the gift. ¹⁷O LORD, your mercy is with all the earth in kindness. ¹⁸Blessed is he whom God remembers with a sufficient sum. ¹⁹When the man was overly wealthy, he caused to sin. ²⁰Sufficient is the measure of righteousness, but in

this is the blessing of the LORD, to be filled in righteousness. ^{21}Those who feared the LORD in prosperity rejoiced when your kindness was upon Israel in your sovereign rule. ^{22}Praised be the glory of the LORD, because he is our King!

PSALM 6
A Psalm of Solomon in Hope.

^{1}Blessed is the man whose heart is fixed to call upon the name of the LORD. ^{2}When he remembers the name of the LORD, he will be saved. ^{3}His roads are paved by the LORD, and the works of his hands are maintained by the LORD, his God. ^{4}His soul is not disturbed by evil visions of his dreams. ^{5}When he passes through rivers and torrential waves, he will not be afraid. ^{6}He rises from his sleep and praises the name of the LORD. ^{7}In the stability of his heart, he exults the name of his God and seeks the face of the LORD for everyone in his house. ^{8}And the LORD hears the prayer of everyone who fears God, and the LORD fulfills every request of the soul that hopes in him. ^{9}Praised be the LORD, who shows mercy to those who love him in truth!

PSALM 7
A Psalm of Solomon Regarding Restoration.

^{1}Do not move away from us, O God, lest those who hate us wrongfully attack us. ^{2}Rather, may you reject them, O God! May their feet not tread your holy temple! ^{3}Chastise us according to your will, but do not give us up to the nation. ^{4}For, if you send death, may you give it order concerning us because you are merciful, and may you not be furious to destroy us together. ⁵While your name dwells in the midst of us, we will receive mercy, ⁶and the nation will not overpower us, because you are our defense. ⁷And we will call to you, and you will listen to us. ⁸For, you will have pity on the seed of Israel forever, and you will not destroy. We are both under your yoke forever and under the rod of your chastisement. ⁹You will direct us in time as you help, when you will have mercy on the house of Jacob, into the day in which you have promised them.

PSALM 8
A Psalm of Solomon for the Chief-Musician.

¹My ear heard distress and the sound of war; it was the sound of trumpet proclaiming slaughter and annihilation, ²the sound of many people as of a very powerful wind, as of the incineration of an awesome fire spreading through a dry place. ³And I said in my heart, "Where will God judge him?" ⁴I heard a sound: "In Jerusalem in the city of the temple." ⁵My guts were destroyed at the hearing; my knees became weak. ⁶My heart became afraid; my bones were shaken like flax. ⁷I said, "They pave their paths in righteousness." I considered God's judgments from the creation of the heaven and the earth, and I declared God as righteous in all of his judgments from eternity. ⁸God revealed their sins before the sun. May all the earth recognize the righteous judgment of God! ⁹Their transgressions in ecstasy were in worldly secrets. ¹⁰Son with mother and father with daughter brought confusion. ¹¹Each committed adultery with his neighbor's wife; they made such alliances with an oath about these things. ¹²They stole the holy place of God; there was not a rightful inheritor to redeem. ¹³They attended to the altar of the

LORD after every unclean act, and in impurity they desecrated the sacrifices like defiled meat. ¹⁴They did not avoid sin, which they did not commit greater than the Gentiles. ¹⁵For this, God mixed for them a spirit of perverseness; he made them drink mixed wine until drunk. ¹⁶He led him from the end of the earth – the one who strikes mightily. ¹⁷He made a judgment of war against Jerusalem and her land. ¹⁸The rulers of the land greeted him with joy and said to him, "Blessed is your path! Come, enter in peace." ¹⁹They fashioned rough paths from their inroad; they opened the gates of Jerusalem; they crowned her wall. ²⁰He entered in like a father into the home of his sons – in peace. He established his feet with great certainty. ²¹He occupied her fortresses and the wall of Jerusalem, ²²because God led him with certainty amidst the blindness of them. ²³He exiled their rulers and every wise man in the assembly. He shed the blood of the residents of Jerusalem like waste water. ²⁴He led away sons and their daughters, whom they conceived in corruption. ²⁵They acted according to their corruption, like their fathers; ²⁶they desecrated Jerusalem and the holy things dedicated to the name of God. ²⁷God has been declared righteous in his judgments among the Gentiles of the earth, ²⁸and the holy men of God are like lambs in innocence in their midst. ²⁹Praised be the LORD who judges everyone on earth in his righteousness. ³⁰Now, behold! O God, you gave us your judgment in your righteousness. ³¹Their eyes saw your judgment, O God. We declared as righteous the virtue of your name, forever. ³²For, you are the God of righteousness who judges Israel in chastisement. ³³O God, turn your mercy toward us and have compassion on us! ³⁴Gather together the diaspora of Israel with mercy and kindness! ³⁵For, your faithfulness is with us. So, we stiffen our neck, and you are our chastiser. ³⁶O our God, do not overlook us, lest the people consume us with none delivering. ³⁷And you are our God from the beginning, and we hope in you, O LORD. ³⁸We did not depart from you because your judgments on us are kind. ³⁹To us and our children is the good-will for eternity, LORD our Savior. We still will not be shaken for eternal time. ⁴⁰Praised is the LORD for his judgments in the mouth of the holy ones! ⁴¹And you are blessed, Israel, by the LORD for eternity!

PSALM 9
A Psalm of Solomon for Chastisement.

¹When Israel was exiled in captivity into a strange land, when they stood away from the LORD who redeemed them, ²they were ripped away from their inheritance which the LORD gave to them into every people, in the diaspora of Israel according to the Word of God, ³so that you might be declared righteous, O God, in your righteousness in our sins. ⁴For, you are a righteous judge over all people of the earth. ⁵Indeed, all who do evil will not be hidden from your knowledge. ⁶And the righteous deeds of your holy ones are before you, O LORD, and where will a man hide from your knowledge? ⁷O God, our works are in our decision and in the power of our soul, to do righteousness or evil in the works of our hands. ⁸And in your righteousness you visit the sons of men. ⁹He who does righteousness saves for himself life according to the LORD, and he who does evil is himself guilty of the soul in destruction. ¹⁰Indeed, the judgments of the LORD are in righteousness against man and house. ¹¹To whom will you be kind, O God, if not to those who call on you? ¹²He will purify the soul in sin when he confesses in acknowledgments. ¹³For, the guilt is on us and on our faces on account of all these.

[14]And for whom will he forsake sins, if not for those who sinned? [15]You will bless the righteous, but you will not make straight for the one who sinned. And your kindness is for sinners in repentance. [16]And now, you are the God, and we are the people whom you love. Look and have pity, O God of Israel, because we are yours! And do not move your mercy from us, lest it is not established upon us. [17]For, you chose the seed of Abraham before all the Gentiles. [18]And you have set your name on us, O LORD, and you will not cease, into eternity. [19]In a covenant, you covenanted with our fathers concerning us, and we trust in you in the turning of our soul. [20]The mercy of the LORD is upon the house of Israel for eternity and evermore.

PSALM 10

A Hymn of Solomon.

[1]Blessed is a man, whom the LORD remembers in chastisement; he is encircled away from the road of evil in affliction, to be cleansed from sin, so that it would not be multiplied. [2]He who prepares his back for whipping will be purified; for, the LORD is kind to those who submit to chastisement. [3]For, he will straighten the paths of the righteous ones, and he will not turn away in chastisement. [4]The mercy of the LORD is upon those who love him in truth; the LORD will remember his slaves in mercy. [5]The witness is in the law of the eternal covenant; the witness of the LORD is in the paths of men in visitation. [6]Righteous and holy is our LORD in his judgments into eternity, and Israel will praise the name of the LORD in joy. [7]And the holy ones will give thanks in the assembly of the people, and God will have mercy on the poor ones in the joy of Israel. [8]For, kind and merciful is God into eternity, and the

ingathering of Israel will glorify the name of the LORD. ⁹The salvation of the LORD is on the house of Israel into everlasting joy.

PSALM 11
Of Solomon into Expectation.

¹Trumpet in Zion with a trumpet of Jubilee for the holy ones! ²Proclaim in Jerusalem the sound of the one proclaiming good news because God had mercy on Israel in the visitation of them. ³Stand up on high, O Jerusalem, and see your children ingathered from the East and the West by the LORD! ⁴From the North, they come in the joy of their God; from distant islands, God has ingathered them. ⁵He flattened lofty mountains into a plain for them. ⁶The hills fled from their entering path; the woods sheltered them in their passage. ⁷Every tree of fragrance God caused to spring up for them, so that Israel might pass by in the visitation of the glory of their God. ⁸Put on, O Jerusalem, the garments of your glory! Prepare the robe of your holy place! For, God has spoken good for Israel into eternity and evermore. ⁹May the LORD do what he has promised concerning Israel and in Jerusalem! May the LORD raise up Israel in the name of his glory! The mercy of the LORD is upon Israel for eternity and evermore.

PSALM 12
Of Solomon on the Tongue of the Transgressors.

¹O LORD, save my soul from the man of transgression and evil – from the tongue of transgression and lying and from the one speaking falsehood and lies! ²In the doing of mis-

leading are the words of the tongue of the evil man; just as the fire on the threshing floor kindles its straw, so is his sojourning, ³to set fire to houses with a false tongue, to remove trees of joy with the enflaming of the transgressing tongue, ⁴to confuse the houses of the transgressors in the war of slandering lips. May God distance from the innocent the lips of the transgressors in poverty, and may the skeleton of the slanderers be scattered away from the fearers of God! ⁵May the tongue of slander be exterminated from the holy ones in the fire of flame! ⁶May God protect the quiet soul who hates unjust ones, and may the LORD guide the man making peace in the house. ⁷The salvation of the LORD is upon Israel, his servant into eternity. ⁸And may the sinners be destroyed away from the face of the Lord, together, and may the holy ones of the LORD inherit the promise of the LORD!

PSALM 13
A Psalm of Solomon, Comfort for the Righteous Ones.

¹The right hand of the LORD covered me; the right hand of the LORD spared us. ²The arm of the LORD rescued us from the sword that passed through, from famine and from the plague of the sinners. ³Wicked beasts ran upon them; with their teeth, they chewed their flesh; and with their jaws they broke their bones. And from all these, the LORD rescued us. ⁴The impious man was troubled because of his violations, lest he might be taken along with the sinners. ⁵For, terrible is the catastrophe of the sinner, and the one of righteousness will not be harmed by all these things – not at all! ⁶For, the chastisement of the righteous ones in ignorance is not the same as the catastrophe of the sinners. ⁷The righteous is chastised in concealment, so

that the sinner might not rejoice over the righteous. [8]For, he will warn the righteous as a beloved son, and his chastisement as of a first-born son. [9]For, the LORD will spare his holy ones, and he will wipe away their violations in chastisement. For, the life of the righteous ones is for eternity. [10]But, the sinners will be taken away into destruction, and the memory of them will no longer be found. [11]But on the holy ones is the mercy of the LORD, and on those who fear him is his mercy.

PSALM 14

A Hymn of Solomon.

[1]Faithful is the LORD to those who love him in truth, to those who endure his chastisement, to those who walk in the righteousness of his commandments, in the law as he commanded us for our eternal life. [2]The holy ones of the LORD will live in it into eternity. The garden of the LORD and the tree of life are his holy ones. [3]Their planting is rooted into eternity; they will not be plucked out all the days of heaven. For, the portion and the inheritance of God is Israel. [4]And such are not the sinners and transgressors, who enjoyed the day in partnership with their sins, in short space of corruption, in their lust. [5]And they did not remember God, that the paths of men are known before him through all, and the private chambers of the heart were known before their being. [6]On account of this, their inheritance is hell and darkness and destruction, and they will not be found in the day of the mercy for the righteous ones. [7]But the holy ones of the LORD will inherit life in joy.

PSALM 15

A Psalm of Solomon with a Song.

¹In my affliction, I called on the name of the LORD; for help, I trusted in the God of Jacob, and I was preserved. ²For, the hope and refuge of the poor ones are you, O God! ³For, who is strong, O God, if not to praise you in truth? ⁴And what is a strong man, if not to give thanks to your name? ⁵A psalm and praise with a song in the joy of the heart, the fruit of the lips with the well-tuned instrument of the tongue, the first-fruit of the lips from a holy and righteous heart. ⁶He who does these will not be shaken by evil into eternity; the flame of fire and the wrath of the unrighteous ones will not touch him, ⁷when it goes out to the sinners from the face of the LORD, to destroy all the standing of the sinners. ⁸For, the mark of God is on the righteous ones for salvation; famine and the sword and the plague are far from the righteous ones. ⁹For, they will flee from the holy ones as the enemy who is being pursued. But it will pursue the sinners and will capture them, and those who work lawlessness will not escape the judgment of the LORD, like those who are captured by warriors of war. ¹⁰For, the mark of destruction is on their forehead. ¹¹And the inheritance of the sinners is destruction and darkness, and their lawlessness will pursue them into Hell below. ¹²Their inheritance will not be found in their children. ¹³For lawless women will destroy the houses of the sinners, and the sinners will perish in the day of the judgment of the LORD into eternity, ¹⁴when God visits the earth in his judgment, to recompense the sinners into eternal time. ¹⁵But those who fear the LORD will find mercy in it, and they will live in the mercy of their God.

PSALM 16

Psalms of Solomon

A Psalm of Solomon for Help.

¹In the inducement of torpor of my soul away from the LORD, in a short time I fell into the heaviness of sleep. ²In being far away from God, after a while my soul poured out into death. I would have been joined to the gates of hell with the sinner, ³in the causation of my soul to depart from the LORD, God of Israel, if the LORD had not helped me in his mercy into eternity. ⁴He pricked me as the spur of a horse so that I might heed him; my savior and helper at all times preserved me. ⁵I will praise you, O God, because you helped me into salvation and did not count me among the sinners into destruction. ⁶Withdraw neither your mercy from me, O God, nor your remembrance from my heart unto death. ⁷Strengthen me, O God, from wicked sins and from every wicked woman snaring the naïve! ⁸May neither the beauty of a transgressing woman enthrall me, nor anything composed of unprofitable sin. ⁹Establish the works of my hands in your word, and preserve my crossing over in your remembrance. ¹⁰Guard my tongue and my lips in the words of truth; make fury and irrational wrath far from me. ¹¹Distance from me grumbling and weak-heartedness! If I sin in this, you chastise me unto restoration. ¹²But uphold my soul with goodwill alongside cheerfulness; in your strengthening of my soul, what you give will satisfy me. ¹³For if you do not strengthen, who will endure the chastisement in poverty? ¹⁴In the faulting of the soul in the hand of his own corruption, your testing is in his flesh and in the affliction of poverty. ¹⁵The righteous man enduring all these things will find mercy from the LORD.

PSALM 17

A Psalm of Solomon with a Song for the King.

¹O LORD, you yourself are our king forever and ever, because in you, O God, our soul exults. ²And what is the time of a man's life on earth? According to his time is also his hope on it. ³But for us, we will hope in God, our savior, because the power of our God is into eternity with mercy. ⁴And the kingdom of our God is into eternity over the Gentiles in judgment. ⁵You, O LORD, chose David king over Israel, and you swore to him regarding his seed into eternity, that his kingdom would not fall before you. ⁶And the sinners rose up against us in our sins; they overtook us and expelled us. You did not promise to them; they took with violence. ⁷And they did not glorify your honorable name in glory; they preferred the throne in place of their exaltation. ⁸They destroyed the throne of David in the pride of triumph-shouting, and you, O God, will thrust them down and remove their seed from the earth, ⁹in the raising up for them a man who is a stranger to our kind. ¹⁰According to their sins, you will repay them, O God. May it be found for them according to their works! ¹¹According to their works, God will show them mercy. He searched for their seed and has not forgiven them. ¹²Faithful is the LORD in all his judgments, which he makes on earth. ¹³The storm wiped out our land from those inhabiting it; it destroyed young and old and their children together. ¹⁴In fury, he expelled his excellent ones from here even into the west and the rulers of the land into derision, and he did not spare them. ¹⁵In alienation, the adversary committed insolence, and his heart was alien from our God. ¹⁶And he did such things in Jerusalem, as also the Gentiles did in the cities for their God. ¹⁷And the sons of the covenant in the midst of the mixed people surpassed them; there was none who practiced mercy and truth among them in the

Psalms of Solomon

midst of Jerusalem. [18]Those who love the gathering of saints fled from them, like sparrows scattering from their nest. [19]They wandered in desert places, to preserve their souls from evil, and precious in the eyes of the sojourning was a soul saved from them. [20]The scattering of them was created into every land by lawless men, so that the heaven stopped dropping rain on the land. [21]Fountains were stopped together with eternal ones from the depths and from high mountains, because there was none among them who did righteousness and justice. From their rulers to the lowest of people were in every sin. [22]The king was in transgression, the judge was in disobedience, and the people were in sin. [23]Look, O LORD, and lift up for them their king, a son of David, into the time you know, O God, to rule over Israel, your slave, [24]and gird him with strength to cast down unjust rulers! [25]Purge Jerusalem from the people who trample – in destruction, in wisdom, and in righteousness! [26]May he expel the sinners from the inheritance; may he annihilate the pride of the sinners; may he break in pieces their substance like the potter's vessels with an iron rod! [27]May he destroy transgressing Gentiles with the word of his mouth, so that at his rebuke Gentiles might flee from his face, and may convict the sinners with the word of his heart! [28]And he will gather together a holy people, whom he will lead in righteousness, and he will judge the tribes of the people, sanctified to the LORD, his God. [29]He will not allow injustice to lodge in their midst, and any man among them knowing evil will not reside. [30]For, he will know them because all will be sons of their God, and he will portion them out in their tribes on the earth. [31]And sojourners and foreigners will not reside with them anymore; he will judge the people and Gentiles in the wisdom of his righteousness. *Selah*. [32]And he will posses peoples of nations to be slaves to him under his yolk, and he will glorify the LORD in conspicuity before all the earth. ³³And he will purge Jerusalem in the sanctuary, as it also was from the beginning. ³⁴Gentiles will come from the end of the earth to see its glory, carrying as gifts her sons who had fainted, ³⁵and to see the glory of the LORD, with which God glorified her. And this righteous king, taught by God, will be over them. ³⁶And there is not injustice in his days in the midst of them, because all are holy, and their king is the anointed of the LORD. ³⁷For, he does not hope in a horse, a rider, and a bow; he does not multiply for himself gold and silver for war; and he will not gather with ships hopes for the day of war. ³⁸The LORD himself is his king, the hope of him who is strong in the hope of God, and he will have mercy on all the Gentiles in fear before him. ³⁹For, he will strike the land with the word of his mouth into eternity. ⁴⁰He will bless the people of the LORD in wisdom with joy. ⁴¹And he himself is pure from sin, in order to rule a great people, to rebuke rulers, and to wipe out sinners in the power of the word. ⁴²And he will not faint in his days with his God, because God caused him to be powerful in holy spirit and wise in the counsel of empathy with strength and righteousness. ⁴³And the blessing of the LORD is with him in power, and his hope in the LORD will not faint. ⁴⁴And who is powerful for him? He is mighty in his works and strong in the fear of God, ⁴⁵tending the flock of the LORD in faith and righteousness, and he will not allow to faint among them in their pasture. ⁴⁶In holiness, he will lead them all, and there will not be among them pride to bring about oppression among them. ⁴⁷This is the majesty of the king of Israel, which God knew: To raise him over Israel, to chastise him. ⁴⁸His words having been purified above fine gold, the first, he will judge the peoples, tribes of the sanctified ones, in gatherings. ⁴⁹His words are like the words of holy ones in

Psalms of Solomon

the midst of sanctified peoples. ⁵⁰Blessed are those born in those days, to see the good of Israel in the gathering of the tribes, which God will do. ⁵¹To rush his mercy on Israel, God will deliver us from the impurities of defiled adversaries. The LORD himself is our king forever and ever!

PSALM 18
A Psalm of Solomon about the Anointed of the LORD.

¹O LORD, your mercy is upon the words of your hands into eternity! ²Your goodness is upon Israel with gifts of plenty; your eyes look upon them, and he will not be in want from them. ³Your ears will heed the prayer of the poor one in hope; your judgment is upon all the earth with mercy. ⁴And your love is upon the seed of Abraham, sons of Israel; your chastisement is upon us as upon the first-born of the only-begotten, ⁵to convert the obedient soul from naiveté in ignorance. ⁶May God purge Israel into the day of mercy in blessing, into the day of appointing in bringing back his anointed! ⁷Blessed are those who will be born in those days, to see the good of the LORD, which he will do for the generation that comes, ⁸by the rod of chastisement of the anointed of the LORD in the fear of his God, in the wisdom of the spirit and of righteousness and power, ⁹to direct mankind in the works of righteousness in the fear of God and to establish them all in the fear of the LORD. ¹⁰A good generation is in the fear of God in the days of mercy. *Selah.*

PSALM 19

[1]Our God is awesome and dwelling glorious in the highest! [2]It is he who decreed the stars for journey into periods of hours from days to days, and they have not strayed away from the path, which he set for them. [3]In the fear of God is their path, every day, from that day when God created them and to eternity. [4]And they have not erred from that day when he created them. From old generations, they did not depart from their path, if God did not command them in the decree of his servants.

Chapter One: The Psalms of Solomon in the Context of Second Temple Jewish History

The Psalms of Solomon, written by a Zadokite priest living in Jerusalem shortly after the Maccabean Revolt in the Second Century BC, is a very important document from the Late Second Temple period (200 BC to 70 AD). In many ways, the Psalms of Solomon can be seen as a quintessentially Jewish document from the Late Second Temple period which reflects the hopes and fears of all who would consider themselves Jews. In a way, therefore, the Psalms of Solomon unifies or reflects the commonality among the diverse sects, or "denominations," of Judaism from the Late Second Temple period.

What was the central unifying theme of all Jews from the Late Second Temple period? Simply put, it can be understood as the value of the Jerusalem Temple and divine ingathering. The Jerusalem Temple held a central place in the hearts and mind of all Jews from the Late Second Temple period. A part of the reason for its value can be attributed to the historical experience of being displaced from the Land of Israel for many years during the Exile. Many Jews – especially, elites, intellectuals, political leaders, and religious figureheads, and business leaders – were forcefully removed from the Kingdoms of Israel and Judah. The Jerusalem Temple was completely destroyed and many of the Jewish residents were decimated without mercy. The national trauma of destruction and displacement came to be symbolized in one institution, that of the Jerusalem Temple. Thus, the restoration of Jews, as individuals or a corporate entity, came to be understood as necessarily tied to the restoration of the Jerusalem Temple, or rebuilding of the Jerusalem Temple.

Writings from the Exile reflect this hope and aspiration. The Book of Ezekiel describes a beautiful Jerusalem Temple that was to be rebuilt. Parts of the Book of Isaiah also reflect this desire and aspiration. The Jerusalem Temple was seen as representative of the Jews as a people. Thus, the Jerusalem Temple acquired the symbolic unity and identity of all those who called themselves Jews. Without the Jerusalem Temple, Jews were a people without a home and identity. Without the Jerusalem Temple, Jews lived in a state of brokenness. For the Jews of the Exile, the Jerusalem Temple represented *tikkun olam*, or healing of all that is broken in the world. The Jerusalem Temple had to be rebuilt if Jews were ever to understand their identity as Jews. Writing after writing reflects a type of "next year in Jerusalem" sentiment in the period of the Exile.

The Exilic emphasis on the Jerusalem Temple as the quintessential symbol of Jewish identity found a lasting impact. The impact of the Jerusalem Temple and the emphasis on correct cultic worship in the Jerusalem Temple are evident in the writings that reflect the historical experience of return to Jerusalem in the account of the building of the Jerusalem Temple. There is careful detail as to how the religious worship and sacrificial cultic practices are to be carried out in the Jerusalem Temple as much as there is stress on the details of the building structure itself. For the Jews of the Exilic period and those who saw return to Zion, the Jerusalem Temple was more than a physical building. The Jerusalem Temple embodied collective hopes and fears of the Jewish people that were attached to understanding their relationship with God. Thus, not only must the Jerusalem Temple be rebuilt but correct cultic worship must also be carried out. The rebuilding of the Jerusalem Temple meant nothing if the correct cultic worship was not carried out.

The understanding that correct cultic worship was at least as important as the physical presence of the Jerusalem Temple can be explained in light of the historical experience of the Jewish people. Jews in the Exile remembered that the Jerusalem Temple was completely destroyed by Gentiles. They remember that there were priests rendering service to the institution of the Jerusalem Temple. There were sacrifices at the appointed times. There were praises sung by the Levites according to the liturgical instructions of the cult. There were Jews attending the Jerusalem Temple service at the gathering times. However, the Jerusalem Temple was still destroyed by the Gentiles.

Writings after writings reflect that Jews in the Exile understood the historical experience of the destruction of the Jerusalem Temple and, in fact, of the country in terms of improper cultic worship. Yes, there were worship services conducted at appointed times, by the book, but they were outward rituals without real content. Furthermore, writings from the Exile explain that the outward form of worship was not accompanied by sincere love or loyalty to God. There was something wrong with the worship services and sacrifices to annoy God and bring down his divine judgement on all Jews, resulting in death of many and displacement of the left over Jews to the Exile out of the Land of Israel.

Many prophetic books in the Old Testament, in fact, bring charges against the institution of the Jerusalem Temple as well as against the Jewish people and political and religious leaders who represented them. The prophets of the Old Testament bring charges against Israel and Judah on three levels, therefore. It was because of the violations of the Jews as a people, Jewish political leaders, and Jewish religious leaders that God brought complete destruction of their country and death of their citizens. God was so angry that He even destroyed the Jerusalem Temple itself, which represented His presence in the Land of Israel and among the people of Israel. The only reason that God did not completely kill all Jews after completely destroying their country and their cities was for His own glory. God wanted a true remnant for Himself to build true worship in the future so that He could receive worship and glory.

The prophets of the Old Testament are systematic in their bringing of accusations against the Jewish people, Jewish political leaders, and Jewish religious leaders. In a sense, therefore, the prophets of the Old Testament should be seen as prosecutors of God bringing an official charge on behalf of God Himself. And the Bible shows that the Jewish people, Jewish political leaders, and Jewish religious leaders are found guilty of the official charges brought against them by the prophets of God in the Old Testament. And the sentence was death and destruction, which was carried out through the agency of God's henchmen. In the case of the destruction of the Jerusalem Temple and the complete destruction of the country where the Jerusalem Temple was found, God's henchmen was King Nebuchadnezzar of Babylon, which is present day Iran and Iraq.

What were the official, recorded charges of God's prosecutors against the three defendants – the Jewish people, Jewish political leaders, and Jewish religious leaders? Against the Jewish people as a whole, the prophets of God brought charges in three main areas: (1) participation in desecrated worship of God, (2) proliferation of economic practices that did not reflect the mercy of God, (3) allowing idolatry and religious plurality to proliferate in public institutions and public spheres. In many ways, these three charges were seen as integrally related by the prosecutors representing God and His rule. But these charges are clearly identifiable in these three separate categories and also even often found separately, so they will be treated as separate charges.

First of all, God's prosecutors bring charge in the case of God versus the People in the realm of religious worship. God's prosecutors accuse the people of participating in desecrated worship of God. It was in their very participation in desecrated religious worship services that they have committed a crime against God worthy of death. The people were going to religious worship services and believed that merely attending these worship services in their appointed times would save them. They believed that they were going to hear the Word of God, and they were, in fact, storing blessings of God by going faithfully to partake of sacraments dispensed through sacrifices and worship services. The prosecutors of God claim that it was their very act of going to worship services and their participation in the sacraments of God that made them guilty because the sacraments were defiled and unacceptable before God and the worship services were desecrated so that they offended God and raised His anger. Thus, the people were charged on being accomplices to offensive sacraments and desecrated worship services that required capital punishment of God. The maximum sentencing on earth on the charge of aiding and abetting desecration of worship and defiling of the sacraments was death.

Why were the sacraments defiled? Why were the sacrifices unacceptable before God? The prosecutors of God level a charge that the sacrifices were unacceptable on the grounds of intent and practice. In terms of intent, the prophets of God argue that the sacrifices were not intended for God. Sacrifices were meant to be performed to glorify God and trust in His redemptive role, but they had become mere forms without faith or heart of love for God. Although they sacrificed, the sacrifices did not result from the purity of heart and belief that God was their true and only Savior. Because the people participating in sacrifices that did not emphasize loyalty to God alone and belief that He is the only Savior, their participation in the sacraments did not result in forgiveness of sins or adding of grace. In fact, they drank and ate God's judgment on themselves through the participation in the sacraments. Instead of adding grace, God added their liability for judgment in each sacrament they partook.

How were religious worship desecrated? Worship services during appointed times were desecrated because of idolatry. The sanctuary of God should be pure of visible political symbols and sharing of devotion and loyalty to anything other than God Himself. But the worship services for God contained privileging of the nation's political interests to gain loyalty to the state. The flag of the nation, so to speak, were placed in the sanctuary of God to remind the worshippers that they are to be loyal to the state. The state tried to associate loyalty to God with the loyalty to the state. Whenever people worshipped God, they were to be reminded by the nation's "flag," that they were to be loyal to the state. They were not to separate their loyalty to God with the loyalty to the state. In fact, it was the very fact of equating the loyalty to God with the loyalty to the state that brought down God's condemnation against the people.

The people were to be loyal to God *against* the state if God demanded. But the worship services were meant as political propaganda by the state to uphold its secular political power so that they could amass more power and control over the people. Because people did not protest the competition of state power against God's power, they were accused. When the people were found guilty, it is no accident that God chose a political power that neither worshipped God nor were saved by Him in spiritual terms to completely decimate the "chosen" people and the "chosen" city and the House of God on earth. God preferred annihilation of God's people, God's city, and God's Temple by those who do not believe or worship Him in any shape or form to sharing his glory with the nation's "flag" during desecrated worship services. God preferred *no* worship to desecrated, or "shared," worship. God wanted silence from those who gathered to "worship" Him by killing them off rather than having them worship with the nation's "flag" in the sanctuary for worship. The people, by participating in the desecrated worship services, were charged with being accomplices to the desecration of worship service for God. The guilty verdict brought the maximum earthly penalty of death, which was delivered by God's "anointed" King Nebuchadnezzar of Babylon.

Besides the case of God versus the People, there were two other cases: God versus Political Leaders and God versus Religious Leaders. In the case of God versus Political Leaders, God's prosecutors leveled a charge of normalizing religious plurality throughout the country. God's prophets accused the political leaders of introducing idolatry to the nation's public spheres and defending the right of idolatry to proliferate in the land and even gain dominance over spheres that were traditionally wholly dedicated to honoring God and God alone. The prophets accused the political leaders of protecting idolatry and actually pushing idolatry unto the population. If it were not for the political leaders and their pushing of idolatry and religious plurality forcibly onto the believing population, the nation would not have become so secularized and odious to God as a nation. It would not have been possible for the nation to be so thoroughly idolatrized and religiously pluralized in all its public and social institutions if political leaders did not legislate against true religion and use the force of the state to impose anti-God laws and traditions upon the populace. The political leaders are blamed for the sorry state of religious pluralism and the proliferation of idolatry in nation's public, social, political, civic, and educational institutions.

There are several reasons why the nation's political leaders have pushed religious pluralism and idolatry in the nation's public, political, civic, social, and educational institutions. One of the reasons was intermarriage. It is a fundamental rule of the Bible that believers not be unequally yoked. But the nation's leaders have married people of other religions. Thus, true religion was diluted in the home of political leaders because they married those belonging to other religions. To accommodate the wife, many political leaders did not emphasize true religion in the home or on the national level. There was widespread intermarriage across religious lines among the elites. The Bible accuses King Solomon of having started the trend that led to the proliferation of idolatry and religious pluralism in the land.

Another reason for the proliferation of religious pluralism and idolatry in the land was due to power issues. Nation's political leaders were afraid of one religion gaining too much power. The political leaders wanted to hold the say in the country and did not want religious leaders interfering in any way or even having the possibility of interfering in any way through their influence. Thus, the nation's political leaders embarked on a power grabbing trip to disenfranchise the nation's religious leaders. They wanted a separation of the church and state so that the state – and its political representatives – would have supreme power and the ultimate say in the adjudication of issues and directing of nation's policies. It was in the interest of political leaders to disenfranchise religions – especially one religion that commands the majority of the populace in terms of worship and group identity. It was in the interests of the political leaders to divide and conquer the people by promoting religious plurality and idolatry. Thus, the power struggle aspect as viewed in terms of church and state dichotomy cannot be overlooked.

Political leaders had something to gain from ensuring that one religion – even true religion (or especially, true religion) – from gaining ascendancy. True religion would hold their actions to account; true religion would require political reforms in light of God's Word. Political leaders did not want to lose their hold on power and the wealth they acquired through various lobbying activities. It is no accident that the prophets of God condemn political leaders of taking bribes and lobby contributions. The prophets of God describe this as violation of God's Law and calls on political leaders and judges to repent. True religion was the only thing that really stood in the way of political leaders enjoying their wealth gained through political corruption, so it is understandable why they would not legislate on behalf of true religion. In fact, it was in their political interest to legislate against true religion to proliferate religious plurality and idolatry in the land.

A third reason why political leaders were pushing religious pluralism and idolatry is that they have been brainwashed through secular and pluralistic learning. Under the rule of King Solomon, a lot of secular knowledge and foreign knowledge entered the land. During the process of intellectual discourse and investigation, a type of pluralistic vision of the world was formed. Heavy influence of foreign knowledge became a part of the nation's curriculum, so much so that the knowledge of the nation's history, founded on Biblical principles, were lost or neglected. Knowledge of the Bible and things of God became secondary. Modern sciences and knowledge were taught and seen as superior to the knowledge of the Bible and God's creative force in history. The nation's elites began to push a secularized and pluralized vision for the world – one which departed from the dictates of God. In fact, the Old Testament describes how the teachings of the Bible were reshaped or changed to fit their pluralistic vision of the world, which included the protection of the rights of idolatry and the freedom even of believers' children to pursue idolatry and choose a false religion over the true religion. The struggles between Prophet Jeremiah and the false prophets detail this struggle.

Most political leaders, having being brought up within the context of pluralized society with its vision for pluralism, including plurality of religions, came to adopt a view with which they were inculcated. Many political leaders were incapable of looking at things from any other way than through the lens of pluralism, and they fought to protect the rights of pluralism of religions. Thus, some of the political leaders could be seen as honest in their intent, but their intent and heart had been corrupted by the anti-God and anti-Bible trends in the intellectual realms, including what would be equivalent to today's seminary professors and religious leaders, whom Jeremiah calls, "false prophets." Many political leaders honestly believed that these seminary professors and religious professors were right. But the ignorance of the law is no excuse. Or in this case, being misguided honestly into the criminal position by seeming prophets of God who were false prophets is no excuse. Thus, God's prophets level the criminal charge against religious leaders of protecting the ascendancy of false religion and their representatives in the land. This sentence carried the maximum earthly penalty on an individual level of death.

But because political leaders are representatives of their nation, their actions have consequence far beyond individual guilt. This was the case in the First Temple Period. God's prosecutors brought the charge of promoting idolatry and religious pluralism at the expense of true religion against the political leaders. But the charge brought against the political leaders is equated to the charge brought against the nation itself. It is, in fact, no different from the case of USA versus Iraq in recent days. USA brought charge against Saddam Hussein. Although the United Nations did not find Saddam Hussein guilty, the United States government did. And when the United States government found Saddam Hussein guilty, they found the State of Iraq guilty and worthy of invasion. The United States government believed that Saddam Hussein's guilt was equated with the guilt of the State of Iraq. This analogy helps to explain the charge of God's prosecutors against the political leaders. When the political leaders are being charged, the whole nation is being charged of the crime. Thus, "punishing" of the political leaders involves punishing of the nation. This explains why God deputized King Nebuchadnezzar of Babylon to invade the "chosen" nation and completely destroy it and kill most of its citizens. God versus the Political Leaders, in fact, represents God versus the State. When the political leaders were found guilty of the crime, God's sentencing involved complete destruction of the nation which they represented.

Besides God versus the People and God versus the Political Leaders, there was yet another case; namely, God versus the Religious Leaders. God's prosecutors accuse the religious leaders of three things: (1) not offering pure worship and sacrifices, (2) supporting nation's political interests rather than God's, (3) promoting idolatry and religious pluralism in the land. First of all, God's prophets accuse the religious leaders of not offering pure worship and sacrifice. Although worship was being conducted in their appointed times, they became mere formalities and excuses to get together. Worshipping God in heart and truth was no longer of concern. It was important merely to have the appointed meetings for the sake of having the meetings. Thus, the pure intent of the worship services was compromised. In fact, the Bible describes the gathering for worship as occasions for gathering to do evil. The accusations of the prosecutors on God's behalf show that God took extreme offense at the misappropriation of God's worship times for selfish human ends. The Bible describes that worship is being done with lips but not with the heart.

Besides the problem of pure intent in worship, there was the problem of desecration of worship and sacrifice. The religious leaders of the time were accused of desecrating the worship of God with idolatry. They brought in idols, whether they were national symbols, like a flag, or religious objects, like Baals, and desecrated true worship and sacrifice. Because the religious leaders participated in idolatrous practices in the context of worshipping God and promoting of national symbols or loyalty to anyone other than God during worship services, the form of worship was corrupted. That worship and sacrifice became unacceptable because of actual physical desecration of the worship service in terms of liturgy or actual practice, displeasing to God. Because the worship services were desecrated, everyone who participated in the worship services was participating in worship unacceptable to God. The participants in desecrated worship services, in fact, became accomplices to the guilt of desecrating worship services for God and incurred charges personally for that. Because it was the religious leaders who pushed desecration of worship services and sacrifices, they were primarily responsible even though religious worshippers and participants were accomplices to the crime against God.

Besides tainting religious worship of God, the nation's religious leaders are charged by God's prosecutors of supporting nation's political interests rather than God's. Obviously, God's rule is not man's rule. Political institutions on earth do not reflect God's rule on earth in most cases. Especially in Israel and Judah, political institutions had gone far away from reflecting God's will for the country. The nation's political leaders were promoting idolatry and religious pluralism and offending God in the process. It was up to the nation's religious leaders to stand opposed to the political leaders for wanting to destroy true worship of God in the country and pushing false religion onto the believing populace by the force of law and their political influence. But religious leaders of the time buckled under pressure. They kowtowed to political pressures from the federal government.

National interests were pushed by the representatives of the government, and religious leaders were expected to comply with the demands of various agencies of the federal and local governments. Instead of standing firm and representing the interests of God and God's Law, many religious leaders submitted to the temporal authority armed with influence, power, wealth, policing agencies, and the military. When political leaders wanted the religious leaders to say that God blesses the nation, religious leaders duly complied and said that God blesses the nation.

During the time of Jeremiah, this was the case. Every single religious leader consulted by political authority stated that God blesses the nation, except for Jeremiah. Thus, political leaders of his day put him in prison. They said that they were the chosen nation and that Jeremiah was committing treason against the chosen nation. Thus, Jeremiah was imprisoned. But it was Jeremiah who was the true representative of God. It was Jeremiah who condemned the practice of peddling political power at religious leaders to extract assurance from the nation's religious leaders that God still blesses the country. It was a political tool meant for political expediency. Political leaders knew that the people would prefer to hear directly from respected religious leaders that God still blesses the country. They knew that this would put the nation at peace and solicit support from the populace for the government. Thus, political leaders worked hard to gain public verbal assurances from nation's prominent religious leaders that God still blesses the country. Obviously, they compromised the things of God for the good of the nation. And God took offense at this. Thus, the prosecutors of God brought charges against the nation's religious leaders for selling out God for nation's political interests and security.

Besides the charge of desecrating pure worship in form as well as in terms of intent and the charge of selling God out for the nation's political interests, the prosecutors of God brought charges against the nation's religious leaders for promoting idolatry and religious pluralism in the land. Prosecutors of God in the Bible deplore the fact that religious leaders of the nation have become the primary conduits through which idolatry and religious pluralism are pushed onto the local population. It was they, the seminary professors of the day and the clergy of the land, who should have fought against idolatry and religious pluralism. But instead, they were participating in promoting false religions and giving them equal status in public discourse and fighting for their right to corrupt true religion. Many in the population were spurred onto idolatry and false religion precisely because of the promotion program of nation's seminaries and clergy. Without the help of the seminaries and the clergy, true religion could have been protected by the populace, but it was precisely because the religious leaders of the land refused to defend the true religion, but instead pushed false religions at the expense of the true religion, using their education, leadership skills, influence, and their religious institutions, that the nation became thoroughly idolatrous in the name of religious pluralism.

Because the religious leaders, who were supposed to defend the true religion, manipulated their entrusted positions as the guardians of the true religion in order to push idolatry and religious pluralism at the expense of true religion, the prosecutors of God pushed for the destruction of the official places of worship. Thus, the Jerusalem Temple had to be destroyed. If the Jerusalem Temple remained, then the religious leaders would continue to offer desecrated worship services unacceptable to God. Furthermore, the fact that the Jerusalem Temple remained in tact seemed to give the notion to the people of the nation as well as to foreigners that God condoned what was going on in the country. Thus, the Jerusalem Temple had to be destroyed to show that God did not tolerate desecrated worship services.

And in the process, priests and clergy of God had to be slaughtered to show that desecrated worship services resulted in divine wrath and judgment. For the prosecutors of God in the Bible, the fact of God's existence was at stake. God's existence would be doubted if the Jerusalem Temple remained in tact and the nation's priests and clergy allowed to offer corrupted sacraments and desecrated worship services. Houses of worship had to be destroyed and clergy administering sacraments and worship had to be killed to bring God glory. Thus, the charge against the religious leaders of the nation was accompanied by the maximum earthly sentence of death for the clergy and priests and the destruction of houses of worship in the nation. The prosecutors of God passed the verdict of guilty, and the capital punishment was to be carried out by God's "anointed" King Nebuchadnezzer. Being an unbeliever, he happily slaughtered the priests who were supposed to represent God and joyfully destroyed the Jerusalem Temple completely, so that not a trace of it remained.

The charges of the prosecutors of God against the people, against the political leaders, and against the religious leaders of the "chosen" nation are well preserved. All in the Exile were able to read the charges and see the sentencing. In fact, the fact that they were living in the Exile was a proof positive that God's verdict was "guilty" in all three cases and that the sentences were being carried out. For them, they did not have the luxury of those living before the fact of judgment to doubt the charges brought by the prosecutors of God. For many of them, they had living memories of suffering and of others who suffered God's wrath and judgment – this living memory passed on for generations. Many Jews in the Exile could point to a relative who was killed at the hand of invading Babylonian armies. Many of them had seen their mother ravaged by Babylonian soldiers triumphant in the invasion or heard of someone's mother being ravaged. The Bible preserved these accounts. It was an integral part of oral and written history of the people that the complete destruction of their nation and their places of worship were due to the fact that correct worship was not done. Yes, the worship services and mass gatherings were held at their appointed times, but they were tainted in form and intent.

Thus, it is not surprising that when the return to Zion actually occurred, the people and their leaders were concerned about not only rebuilding the Jerusalem Temple but offering proper cultic worship there. Unlike the First Temple period residents of Judah and Israel, the Jews of the Second Temple period knew that the physical existence of the "House of God" in the "chosen" city was useless without proper cultic worship service and loyalty to God to whom worship was being offered. The sanctity of the Jerusalem Temple, in fact, could be compromised by improper worship and idolatry. God required obedience and not sacrifice.

Thus, Second Temple literature is concerned with proper cultic worship and effort to ensure that the mistake of the proliferation of idolatry and religious pluralism not occur in the land, leading to the destruction by God of the country and the Holy City and the slaughter of the residents. Thus, it is no surprise that there is strong injunction against intermarriage. Since intermarriage was identified as the source of religious pluralism, the Book of Nehemiah contains a directive that all Jews who married Gentiles divorce their wives. It did not matter if they were true soulmates or true love of their life. It did not matter if they were the most important people in their life. It did not matter if they were the mother of their beloved children. It did not matter if they saved their life or provided the joy of their lives. The rule was simple and that was that all Jews were to divorce Gentile wives. Thus, believers were not to be unequally yoked. Not only should believers not enter into marriage with non-believers. They were to divorce non-believing wives. This represents one conscious effort in the period of the Second Temple period to not repeat the mistakes of the First Temple period. But there were many such measures in the Second Temple period.

    Such measures of prevention of idolatry and religious pluralism in the land must be seen through the experience of the charges of the prosecutors of God in the First Temple Period against the people, their political leaders, and the religious leaders, and in the carrying out of the punishment ensuing from the guilty verdicts. Israel and Judah were completely destroyed. What they imagined not possible – complete destruction – happened for the first time in their history as a people since Exodus. In fact, it was the first time such thing happened since the founding of the nation. No one imagined that the country could be completely destroyed so that there ceased to be a nation in any sense of that word. The unimaginable happened. Returning from the unimaginable generations after the fact, those in the Second Temple period were determined to safeguard against a reoccurrence.

    The concerns of the beginning part of the Second Temple period is found in the Late Second Temple period as well. The Jerusalem Temple was seen as the most important institution and the primary symbol of the Jewish people. And like the spirit of the beginning part of the Second Temple Period, Late Second Temple Period writings exhibit that they understood the legitimacy of the Jerusalem Temple Period depended on proper cultic worship and excising of idolatry and religious plurality from the land. The memory of the trauma of the Exile fastened the symbiotic identity of the Jerusalem Temple and proper cult in the collective consciousness of all in the land and in the Diaspora.

    The Psalms of Solomon represents a summary of the value of the Late Second Temple period common to all Jews. The Psalms of Solomon may have been composed in a sectarian setting or by an individual but it is quintessentially reflective of the concerns of the Late Second Temple Period. The Jerusalem Temple was the most important symbol and institution of the Jewish people and its survival and the survival of the Jewish people depended on its purity and proper cultic worship.

Chapter Two: The Psalms of Solomon in the Context of Late Second Temple Period Jewish Denominations

The Late Second Temple Period, roughly outlined to be from 200 BC to 70 AD, bears a distinctive imprint of the hopes and fears of the Exilic Period and the beginnings of the Second Temple Period. During the Exilic Period, Jews who survived the slaughter of the Babylonians, the destruction of the Jerusalem Temple and the city of Jerusalem, and the complete dismantling of the nation, desired the rebuilding of the Jerusalem Temple and ingathering of the Jews to Jerusalem that would lead to the rebuilding of the Jerusalem Temple. Exilic Jews knew that the new Jerusalem Temple had to be not only a building where religious worship and sacrifices were carried out in form but also a place where pure worship and right cultic practices must guide the administration of the religion. They knew that mere physical presence of the House of God did not mean much, since the House of God was completely destroyed by the Babylonians – heathen unbelievers who were deputized by God to destroy the Jerusalem Temple for improper worship. Form meant nothing without content. Thus, the Second Temple was rebuilt with concern for proper worship and correct cultic practices.

Concern for proper worship and correct cultic practices permeates throughout the literature of the Second Temple period, including most important documents from the Late Second Temple period. In fact, the concern for proper worship and correct cultic practices was so dominant in the period that it was an overriding principle. In other words, there was no other value more important than the idea that proper worship and correct cultic practices should be done in the Jerusalem Temple. Even the concept of the unity of Jews as a people took second place to the overriding principle of cultic purity and correct worship. The Late Second Temple period, in fact, became a test ground of this overriding principle.

In the Late Second Temple period, the Jerusalem Temple was compromised with infiltration of Hellenism. Events leading up to the Maccabean Revolt attest to how pervasive Hellenism was even in the Land of Israel. Greek language and culture became important especially for the elites of the land. After the victory of Alexander the Great and the dividing up of the region among his generals, the whole area experienced an infiltration of Greek language and ideas. It was an active process to go hand in hand with the control that the Greek generals wanted in the areas which they controlled. The occupied territories were not Greek, but the occupiers were Greek. Thus, systematic inculcation of Greek ideas and language was seen as a way to cultural domination and control that would facilitate political and economic control. The Land of Israel was caught up in this whole process of Hellenization, so it is not surprising that there was pervasive Hellenism in the land.

Hellenism was so pervasive and thorough that even Jerusalem's priests and religious leadership were influenced by Hellenism. In fact, the highest leadership in the Jerusalem Temple was thoroughly Hellenized by the Late Second Temple period. There were high priests using Greek names instead of Hebrew names. The interesting fact is that their use of Greek names assumes that they presumed that the local population did not have a problem with the High Priest of the Jerusalem Temple using a Greek name instead of a Hebrew name. This certainly describes the extent of Hellenization. For the local population not to care about their highest religious authority, a person whose authority is akin to the Pope of the Roman Catholic Church, receiving the name of what was seen as enemy Gentile nation shows the extent to which the Jewish populace in the Land of Israel was thoroughly Hellenized. This is especially significant in light of the fact that name has significant and symbolic value in the Old Testament. Names in the Old Testament not only characterized a person vis-à-vis each other, they often described the relationship between the people and God, especially when the name belonged to a representative leader of the people. And the High Priest was the highest religious authority in the land. Furthermore, names in the Old Testament often were used as a prophetic fulfilment. In other words, names were given to leaders as a prophecy of the people during that leader's lifetime. Thus, names in the Old Testament were seen to be sacred and ominous. For the local population to be apathetic to the Hellenistic name of the High Priest meant that they were quite receptive of Hellenism, even in their deepest religious piety.

But not everyone was willing to go along with the process of Hellenization which seemed to have tacit approval at the highest levels of religious leadership in the Land of Israel. There was resistance and resistance gained greater and greater momentum in the Late Second Temple period. In fact, the resistance went from discontent among a few, informally expressed, to organized resistance. In fact, it is in the Late Second Temple period that the phenomenon of denominationalism in Judaism was born.

The overriding principle inherited from the period of the Exile was that mere form of the Jerusalem Temple did not matter. What was important was that there was content to the form. There had to be proper cultic worship in the Jerusalem Temple to enjoy the blessing of God. Obviously, Hellenism was not consistent with the teachings of the Old Testament. Hellenism emphasized plurality and tolerance where the Old Testament Law demanded ritual observance and purity. There were more than a few who realized the deviation of the Jerusalem Temple leadership from the normative Old Testament principle, and they were going to do something about it.

However, the reform tendencies among the Jewish populace remained only at the individual level for decades. There were some individuals discontent at what was going on in the Jerusalem Temple and the process of Hellenism that pervaded that arena, but many found it difficult to attack the Jerusalem Temple directly or effectively. One of the reasons for this is that the Jerusalem Temple held important symbolic power. Many people saw the Jerusalem Temple as the source of redemption. It represented a return from the Exile. It was for many Jews a blessing of God. They were ingathered from Gentile lands and gathered to the land of the promise. For them, the Jerusalem Temple was a physical and tangible proof of God's faithfulness to them and the covenant. God brought them to the land which He showed them to worship Him in His House. Even those with reform tendencies participated in collective valuing of the Jerusalem Temple. It was a hard habit to break. To oppose the physical Jerusalem Temple that was standing proved to be more difficult than they thought. But all this was to change.

One historical event brought individual discontent to the collective level. Ironically, that historical event was the desecration of the Jerusalem Temple by Antiochus IV Epiphanes, the ruler of Syria. It was a foreign invasion that emboldened the reformers among the Jews. Antiochus IV

Epiphanes desecrated the Jerusalem Temple by sacrificing a pig on the altar. Furthermore, Antiochus IV Epiphanes forbade keeping of Sabbath among the Jews. Prohibiting public celebration of one of the most important religious holidays was too much for the Jewish population to bear. Every Jew in the land was affected by the prohibition for public celebration of the important day. Thus, collective discontent was born. And the visible collective discontent emboldened reformist leaders to tap into popular power.

Thus, it is no accident that Judas Maccabaeus raised the banner of religious purity as he wielded his sword to kill Syrian soldiers. Not unlike the American Revolution, people who had never fought in a war before – civilians who used to go about their day and take care of the business of living – took up weapons, learned to fight on the go, and killed soldiers who represented a corruptive force and desecration of true worship. Surprisingly, the Maccabean Revolt was successful. The victory was not anticipated just as the American Revolution, which was called "The Presbyterian Rebellion" at the time by the British, proved to be victorious against all calculations of the British Empire.

The actual war against the Syrians had the ironic effect in several ways. First of all, the war, which was represented as a war against Hellenism, disenfranchised Jewish leaders, including the High Priest, who supported Hellenism. The Hellenistic monarch of Syria desecrated the Jerusalem Temple in the name of Hellenism. The particularity that the Jerusalem Temple represented went against religious pluralism emphasized by Hellenism. In other words, the Jerusalem Temple was desecrated so that religious tolerance which was consistent with the spirit of Hellenism could pervade. From the Hellenistic perspective, it was a good thing that was done. Destroying particularism of the Jerusalem Temple and hindering the specific celebration of a religious day was consistent with the spirit of religious tolerance and religious pluralism. Perhaps, the Hellenized High Priest of the Jerusalem Temple did not buy fully into the program of Hellenism that embraced universalism and religious tolerance to such an extent. However, the Jewish High Priest was a champion of Hellenism in the Land of Israel. In fact, dominant Hellenistic powers of the day expected this of the High Priest and of the people whom he guided. And to a large extent the Hellenized Jewish High Priest fulfilled his obligations to Hellenistic powers faithfully and effectively. When the Jerusalem Temple was desecrated by Hellenistic powers, however, the Jewish High Priest lost all of his legitimacy as the religious head of the Jewish people. Not only did such horrific desecration of the Jerusalem Temple happen under his watch, the High Priest was, in fact, identified with Hellenistic influence in the Land of Israel.

Thus, the desecration of the Jerusalem Temple provided the ideal opportunity for the reformist leaders to oppose the Jerusalem Temple's current leadership and galvanize the Jewish population, in effect, against them. Although the Maccabean Revolt is often described as the resistance of the Jews against the Gentiles who desecrated the Jerusalem Temple, the reality was that it was precisely the political capital needed by the opposition to dethrone the Jewish High Priest and His "political party." For the reformers, some of whom were not above political aspiration for power and wealth that went along with that power, the "foreign" invasion was a gift of God from Heaven.

It is important to remember why it was so difficult for the current Jerusalem Temple leadership to be displaced. Not only were they a part of the current Jerusalem

Temple leadership, they were, in fact, the legitimate priests. These priests and the High Priest may have been Hellenized, but they were still Zadokite priests. And the tradition had it that the Jerusalem Temple must be occupied by Zadokie priests. This was a part of the spirit of correct cultic observation. A Zadokite priest being the High Priest of the Jerusalem Temple dignified the Jerusalem Temple programs as legitimate programs. Since Zadokites were in power, their "political party" – which in their case was their blood-kin and those related to them by marriage – had a vested interest in keeping the Zadokites in power. Fortunately for the Zadokites, they did not merely have the larger clan system operating for them; they had the weight of tradition behind them. Zadokites were the legitimate High Priests. This almost gave them impenetrable power. They had *potestas* coupled with *auctoritas*.

But no earthly power is bullet-proof. The desecration of the Jerusalem Temple by the representative of Hellenism was the silver bullet that did the Zadokites in. Since the Zadokites had been identified with Hellenism and Hellenistic influences in Jerusalem for so long, they were effectively seen as being at fault for what happened in Jerusalem. Since the desecration of the Jerusalem Temple and prohibition of public celebration of a religious holiday trumps any tradition or power attached to a person or groups of people, the Zadokites effectively lost their *auctoritas*. The Zadokites were no longer seen as the legitimate priests for the position of the High Priest. And the political party of the Zadokites came to be identified with corruption of religious pluralism and all moral failings attached to the desecration of the true religion. This paved the way for the rise of the opposition and an opportunity for a new kind of *Fuhrer* to reign in the land.

Not surprisingly, the party to gain complete ascendancy was the political party that pushed for reforms and moral purity and bringing back of the true religion in the land. The Maccabean Revolt lasted only a short period of time, but it was victorious. And the victory against Hellenism soon produced new leadership in the Jerusalem Temple. Zadokite High Priests were completely disenfranchised and their political party absolutely discredited. None among their ranks would ever rise again. The rule of the opposition began in earnest and occupied the land for over a century. The platform that promised bringing pure worship and correct cultic practices was more powerful than any other tradition or laws. This is not surprising because pure worship and correct cultic practices were an overriding principle inherited from years and years of being in the Exile among the Jewish population that was convinced that the legitimate Jerusalem Temple was destroyed because of violations of pure worship and correct cultic practices. Legitimacy of the physical temple mattered not at all when form was devoid of content.

In the same way, the Zadokite priests may be the legitimate priests, but form devoid of content mattered not at all. It was better to have a non-Zadokite priest, who may not be the legitimate High Priest by the forms of tradition but who offered pure worship and correct cultic observations, than a legitimate Zadokite priest who allowed the Jerusalem Temple to be desecrated in the worst way possible and for public celebration of religious holiday to be prohibited. They preferred a new *Fuhrer* who would purify the land and bring back the favor of God so that they could avoid the Exile or any other destructive punishment of God.

Thus, the Hasmonean dynasty was born. The Hasmonean dynasty must, therefore, be seen as a denomination. They deviated from normative Judaism that emphasized that a Zadokite priest must be the High Priest of the Jerusalem Temple. The rise of the Hasmonean dynasty is comparable to a successful Reformaton, in which Martin Luther becomes the Pope of the Roman Catholic Church. There would not be a Protestant church. The Roman Catholic Church would have been shaped according to the vision of Martin Luther. And that's exactly what happened in the Jerusalem Temple. The Hasmoneans shaped the Jerusalem Temple according to their vision for the Jerusalem Temple. One of the Hasmonean vision was combining the priesthood with the monarchy. Thus, Hasmonean priests became kings and queens in the Land of Israel. This certainly is not consistent with the Old Testament vision for the Jerusalem Temple. They fragrantly opposed the principles of the Old Testament once they secured their power in the Jerusalem Temple. But even from the beginning, their support of a non-Zadokite high priest must be seen as a deviation from the received tradition or the creation of a new denomination within "normative" Judaism.

Although new denomination took over the Jerusalem Temple, the legitimate Zadokite high priests were not going to give up. In fact, they believed that their legitimacy as the High Priest of the Jerusalem Temple was so important that they were convinced that people would follow them out of the Jerusalem Temple, now occupied by illegitimate priests, to a new temple they would construct. Zadokite priests, therefore, pictured themselves as the reform party, and their platform was the preservation of the right priesthood. In fact, they tried to fashion their propaganda along the lines that the Jerusalem Temple was not conducting proper worship and observing correct cultic practices because they had illegitimate priests.

Using their reform platform, the Zadokites set up a Jewish temple in Leontopolis in Egypt. The fact that they set them up as the reformers and actually constructed a competing temple to the Jerusalem temple actually made them into a denomination. Thus, the Zadokites became a denomination just like the Hasmoneans. They did not represent "normative" Judaism but a denomination based on their vision for reform. Unfortunately for the Zadokites, the horror of the desecration of the Jerusalem Temple and the prohibition of the public celebration of religious holidays was too much for the Jews to bear. The Zadokites may be legitimate priests but they let the Hellenizers in and commit such atrocious acts in the Land of Israel. In essence, the Jewish people were not willing to forgive the Zadokites for what they thought the Zadokites allowed to be done in the Promised Land. Furthermore, the Zadokites made a grave mistake of constructing a temple in Egypt. Egypt was often associated with dispersion and not ingathering. Since the Exilic period instilled in the hearts of Jews the desired to be gathered in Jerusalem for proper cultic worship, they were not willing to follow even the legitimate priests to a place that represented the Exile, the dispersion, and a state of God's wrath. Thus, the Zadokite temple withered away and eventually disappeared.

The Zadokites and the Hasmoneans were not the only Jewish denominations resulting from the Maccabean Revolt. There were many other denominations. And all these Jewish denominations shared one common factor – emphasis on the Jerusalem Temple and pure cultic worship.

Even among the Zadokites, another Jewish denomination was born. That denomination was the Qumran community. The Qumran community's identity as composed of a Zadokite priest and his followers has been widely discussed. *The Thanksgiving Psalms* (1QH and 4QH) are seen as describing the struggle of the Teacher of Righteousness, a legitimate Zadokite priest, with the Wicked Priest, the current priest at the Jerusalem Temple, who actually drove out the Teacher of Righteousness from Jerusalem. Other Qumran documents, such as *The Children of Light versus the Children of Darkness*, describe not only the historic struggle but the planned military conflict that was to come in the future. *The Temple Scroll* describes the Jerusalem Temple and emphasized proper cultic observation in the Jerusalem Temple. Thus, the Qumranites under the leadership of the legitimate Zadokite priest, called the Teacher of Righteousness, envisioned the day that they would return to Jerusalem and occupy the rightful place in the Jerusalem Temple which was the right of the Zadokite priest. In this sense, the Qumran community represented a Jewish denomination that was interested in religious reforms.

It is important to emphasize that there was no Jewish denomination that did not emphasize the necessity of the Jerusalem Temple and proper cultic worship. The force of the collective experience of the Exile was too much to ignore this overriding principle in any reform policy. One could not call oneself a Jew apart from the Jerusalem Temple. And no religious leader could call himself a religious leader of the Jews if he denigrated the Jerusalem Temple as a redemptive value for the Jews in principle. The Zadokites built a competing Jewish temple in Leontopolis in Egypt, but this must be seen a temporary measure until the Jewish people came to their senses and invited the Zadokites back to be the High Priest of the Jerusalem Temple.

Psalms of Solomon

The Zadokites who refused to participate with their brethren who built a temporary temple in Leontopolis stayed closer to home in Qumran so that they would be more accessible to Jerusalem and could go more readily to take the reign of control from the Wicked Priest and the Hasmonean dynasty when they fell. Both of the Zadokite Jewish denominations emphasized the Jerusalem Temple and proper cultic worship. Like the Zadokite denominations, the Hasmonean denomination, too, emphasized the Jerusalem Temple and proper cultic worship there. But they were different from the Zadokites in that the Hasmoneans argued that the very act of the desecration of the Jerusalem Temple and the Hellenistic policy of prohibiting public celebration of the religious holiday effectively took away the legitimacy to be the High Priest from the Zadokites. For the Hasmoneans, reform involved a new priestly family, a position they were happy to occupy.

Not all Jewish denominations were set up at the highest level of conflict around the office of the High Priest. One can argue that the three parties discussed above involved primarily priests in leadership and the priests had a vested interest in the struggle. In fact, the winners of the struggle could actually become high priests. But there were other Jewish denominations that were formed with a reform platform that had really no opportunity *per se* for the office of the High Priest. One such denomination is that of the Pharisees. There were priests among the Pharisees, but the predominant membership of the Pharisees was laity. In a sense, therefore, the Pharisees can be seen as lay movement rather than a movement of the clergy. In this sense, the Pharisees represented a completely different kind of a Jewish religious denomination. In fact, the Pharisees represented a new kind of Jewish religiosity – a religiosity with power localized in the laity.

However, it must be emphasized that the Pharisees never denigrated the Jerusalem Temple.

For the Pharisees, the Jerusalem Temple's redemptive value was a given. It was assumed that all good Pharisee would participate actively in the life of the Jerusalem Temple and fulfil its demands. A Jewish denomination was not a Jewish denomination if it denigrated the redemptive value of the Jerusalem Temple in principle. As laity (or predominantly laity) with no possibility of attaining the office of the High Priest or any of the priestly offices, the Pharisees focused on lay-centered organization. Thus, the synagogues were the places of highest Pharisee activity. Synagogues allowed laity to come together and for the laity to participate in leadership.

To facilitate the emphasis on laity-based reforms, the Pharisees encouraged devotion to the Mosaic Law. The Mosaic Law had to be observed by all Jews, whether priest or laity. So, the Pharisees were opportunists who came in and filled the gap created in the process of priest-on-priest conflict. The neglected laity represented most of the population in the Land of Israel, and they were looking for guidance in the midst of confusing conflicts between powerful priestly families of the Zadokites and nouveau powerful priestly family of the Hasmoneans. Which priestly family was to be believed?

The Pharisees emphasized that the Law of God had to be the guide. Thus, they emphasized the reading of the Torah and putting it in daily practice. As the Pharisees filled the gaps created by the clergy, the lay reform movement grew and quickly became a power to contend with. The Hasmoneans either chose to be on their side or oppose them. Thus, even from the Hasmonean dynasty, there is a record of massacre of the Pharisees by one Hasmonean royalty and privileging them as a co-ocperative voice by another Hasmonean royalty. Like today, various Jewish denominations in the Late Second Temple Period made alliances, and sometimes this involved making alliances against other Jewish denominations.

Beside the Pharisees, there were other laity-oriented Jewish denominations in the Late Second Temple Period. The Zealots represent one such group. The Zealots were extremely religious individuals, mostly from among non-priestly Jews, who were dedicated to preserving of religious purity by violent means. They attributed their spirit directly to Judas Maccabee, whose Jewish religious devotion was described as his zeal to kill on behalf of Judaism. Zealots tapped into the Old Testament for examples of religious zeal evidenced in killing to preserve pure religion as inspiration.

The Zealots gained greater momentum as the Hasmonean dynasty began to degenerate and lose their religious emphasis and moral lustre. And the Zealots especially rose to prominence as the Romans came to control Palestine with the ascendancy of the Roman Empire. The Zealots were laity who combined religious devotion with political (and military) activism to ensure that the land remained pure and devoted to correct ritual observance. Zealots as a religious denomination has not been discussed much and more studies will need to be conducted in the future especially in terms of their belief system, social identity, and their relationship with other Jewish denominations.

Besides the two laity denominations – the Pharisees and the Zealots – which did not concern themselves with the power struggles for the High Priesthood, there was a priestly denomination that also did not concern themselves with the High Priesthood. That priestly denomination is the Sadducees. The Sadducees were a priestly group that operated mostly in the context of the Jerusalem Temple. For some reason, the Sadducees are not described as having interest in the position of the High Priest or in trying to attain the highest power in the land. It seemed like the Sadducees were content in their position as a religious denomination, which had a say in the direction of the nation. They seemed to curry favor with the High Priest and the court. And they were found in struggle with the Pharisees in this regard. But they seemed to be content with a position of influence, rather than being in positions of direct power. Perhaps, the Sadducees could be likened unto the House of the Lords in England during traditional days. The Sadducees were priestly individuals from noble families. They can be seen as types of landed gentry or nobles with rank. It seems that it was not possible to join the Sadducees as one joined the Pharisees. Thus, one had to be born into the Sadducees.

    Out of all the Jewish denominations at the time, the Sadducees seemed most visibly Hellenized. Perhaps, they had the luxury to be outwardly Hellenized because their group was somewhat closed to outsiders and they were not interested in gaining too much power. They were happy to remain in their positions of aristocracy. It seems that as long as they had the favor of the court, they were content. In terms of ideas, they show marked liberal tendency that is missing among other Jewish denominations of the time.

    However, the Sadducees were definitely a Jewish denomination in that they privileged the Jerusalem Temple and, in theory at least, emphasized correct cultic worship. The Sadducees showed their support for the Jerusalem Temple most visibly, perhaps, by their physical presence and activity around the temple precincts. As a more or less purely priestly denomination, the Sadducees were of value to the Hasmonean royal dynasty and the religious "denomination" created by the Hasmoneans, which was purely priestly. Although the Sadducees did not seem to be a part of the Hasmonean priestly family, they seemed to be supportive of the Hasmonean dynasty throughout the Late Second Temple Period. This suited the Hasmoneans well since as Hasmoneans became more and more political after taking the role of the monarch of the Land of Israel, they needed more priestly types who were more attached to the Jerusalem Temple and were seen as more purely religious leaders. The Sadducees, therefore, lent priestly credibility to the Hasmonean dynasty.

The Late Second Temple Period became a breeding ground for Jewish denominationalism. New Jewish denominations cropped up, here and there. And all Jewish denominations were somehow entangled in the complex maze of religious institutions and political institutions, which, in fact, became entangled in complex permutations. Despite the diversity of Jewish denominations – which differed in composition and emphasis – there was a commonality to all Jewish denominations. In fact, it would be impossible to call a group Jewish if it missed this unifying and common factor. And this unifying Jewish factor was the Jerusalem Temple and proper cultic worship in that temple. In principle, there was not a single Jewish group that denied this overriding principle of the Jews.

Those who were in the Jerusalem Temple claimed to be legitimately there to conduct proper cultic worship after the previous priests participated in desecrating the temple. The Zadokite denomination that opposed the Hasmonean denomination argued that they were legitimate and set up a make-shift temple and waited for the day that the legitimate priesthood would be restored to the Jerusalem Temple and proper cultic worship be reinstated. Another wing of the Zadokites created their own Jewish denomination in Qumran and described themselves as preparing for the day that the LORD would Himself restore them to the Jerusalem Temple. After the epic battle that would be fought on the ground, the Zadokites could purify the Jerusalem Temple of non-Zadokites and improper cultic practices and restore pure worship and correct cultic observance. The two laity groups – the Pharisees and the Zealots – both emphasized the value of the Jerusalem Temple and focused on the laity in their midst to be more loyal to the pure idea of the Jerusalem Temple and correct cultic observance. And the Sadducees – a priestly denomination not belonging really to the Zadokites or the Hasmoneans – were mostly aristocrats who wanted to survive the storms of the times and maintain their privileged places in society. Certainly in print, the Sadducees privileged the Jerusalem Temple and proper cultic worship in the Jerusalem Temple. They showed their greatest support for the Jerusalem Temple by their daily activities and work around the Jerusalem Temple.

In the Late Second Temple Period, to be a Jew meant to privilege true worship and cultic ritual observance with the Jerusalem Temple at the center. To oppose this ideal was not to be a Jew. No Jewish group could call itself a Jewish group which opposed the Jerusalem Temple in principle. It is in this context that the Psalms of Solomon was composed and passed on. The Psalms of Solomon, therefore, represents the hopes and fears of the Jews of the Late Second Temple Period. In fact, the Psalms of Solomon is a quintessentially a Late Second Temple Period Jewish document. The main emphasis of the Psalms of Solomon reveals the commonality of all Jewish groups of the time – namely, the redemptive value of the Jerusalem Temple and the emphasis on proper worship and correct cultic observance at the Jerusalem Temple.

Chapter Three: The Psalms of Solomon as a Quintessential Late Second Temple Document

The Psalms of Solomon is a quintessential Late Second Temple Period document. What makes the Psalms of Solomon representative are the ideas contained therein. The central ideas of the Psalms of Solomon can be identified as the centrality of the Jerusalem Temple and proper cultic practices. This emphasis is a common value of the Late Second Temple Period for all Jews and all Jewish groups. The reason that the centrality of the Jerusalem Temple and proper cultic observance became the overriding principle was that the Jews of the Second Temple Period were keenly aware of the trauma of the Exile. It was a shock to the Jews that the House of God – namely, the Jerusalem Temple – in the Holy City of Jerusalem could be completely destroyed by Gentile soldiers who did not even believe in God. The trauma of the Exile raised questions about the validity of the covenant of God. Thus, the Second Temple Period Jews sought to find answers for why the House of God was destroyed by Gentiles and the nation completely annihilated and the remnant sent into exile. The conclusion was that the House of God was destroyed because God removed His presence from the House. And God removed His presence from the House of God because the Jews broke the covenant. When the presence of God was removed from the House of God, the city of Jerusalem lost its protection by God. But not only did God remove His presence from the Jerusalem Temple and the city of Jerusalem because the Jews broke the covenant by participating in desecrated worship services and conducted improper cultic practices. Thus, God actually militated against the Jews and their dwelling places, including the city of Jerusalem, by sending foreign invaders in and giving them success to conquer the capital city and absolutely destroy the country. Thus, the Second Temple Period Jews were sensitive to proper cultic practices surrounding the Jerusalem Temple so that they would not again invite God's departure from the House of God in Jerusalem and God's retaliatory response against the Jews for desecration of worship and of the Jerusalem Temple, which would involve death of many Jews, destruction of the capital city, annihilation of the populace, complete dismantling of the nation, and the Exile. The overriding principle of the Second Temple Period is imprinted on the pages of the Psalms of Solomon, a quintessential Late Second Temple Period Document.

As a quintessential Late Second Temple Period Document, the Psalms of Solomon reminds the reader of the trauma of the destruction of Jerusalem and the Exile. Psalms of Solomon 9:1-3 state:

> ^{1}When Israel was exiled in captivity into a strange land, when they stood away from the LORD who redeemed them, ^{2}they were ripped away from their inheritance which the LORD gave to them into every people, in the diaspora of Israel according to the Word of God, ^{3}so that you might be declared righteous, O God, in your righteousness in our sins.

The writer of Psalms of Solomon clearly emphasizes that God was righteous. God was righteous and kept His part of the covenant by giving the inheritance which He had promised to Abraham to His descendants. But it was the Jews who violated the covenant and lost the inheritance. It was the Jews who first departed from the LORD who redeemed them and not the other way around. The Exile was the punishment for the violation of the covenant by the Jews. The psalmist further explains that if God did not send the Jews into exile, then He would not be righteous. The composer of the Psalms of Solomon indicates that it was consistent with God's character of righteousness to destroy Israel and send Jews into the Exile for their violation of the covenant.

The trauma of the Exile had created a lasting fear in the minds of the Jews of the Second Temple Period. Remembering the destruction of Israel by the Gentiles and the Exile, Jews of the Second Temple Period believed that what happened before could happen again. Just as God had removed His presence away from His House out of anger for improper cultic practices and desecrated worship at the Jerusalem Temple during the time of the Babylonians, God could remove His presence again in the current generation. This fear of the Jews of the Late Second Temple Period is stated clearly in Psalms of Solomon 7:1-3:

> ^{1}Do not move away from us, O God, lest those who hate us wrongfully attack us. ^{2}Rather, may you reject them, O God! May their feet not tread your holy temple! ^{3}Chastise us according to your will, but do not give us up to the nation.

Because the Jews of Isaiah and Jeremiah's time were "given over" to the Gentiles, the composer of the Psalms of Solomon believed that this could happen again. The psalmist repeats this fear in Psalms of Solomon 8:36: "O our God, do not overlook us, lest the people consume us with none delivering." The fear of the repetition of the precedent of the Exile was resident in the collective memory of the Jews of the Late Second Temple Period.

Even events occurring during the life-time of the composer of the Psalms of Solomon receives reflection on the collective traumatic experience of the Exile. Psalms of Solomon 8:1 states: "My ear heard distress and the sound of war; it was the sound of trumpet proclaiming slaughter and annihilation." The following verses explain this sound of war to be a real one involving a mighty army. This sound of war was heard in the city of Jerusalem. Psalms of Solomon 8:4-5 states:

> [4]I heard a sound: "In Jerusalem in the city of the temple." [5]My guts were destroyed at the hearing; my knees became weak.

These verses show that the experience was personal. In other words, the composer of the Psalms of Solomon actually experienced a sound of war in Jerusalem. He was a witness to the war in Jerusalem. And based on the collective memory of the destruction of Jerusalem by Gentiles and the ensuing Exile, the composer of the Psalms of Solomon declares the invading Gentile soldiers as righteous. Psalms of Solomon 8:7 states:

> [7]I said, "They pave their paths in righteousness." I considered God's judgments from the creation of the heaven and the earth, and I declared God as righteous in all of his judgments from
> eternity.

As one who remembered God's use of Gentile armies to destroy the Jerusalem Temple and the nation of Israel, the composer of the Psalms of Solomon recognized the potential pattern of God using Gentile soldiers to destroy Jerusalem again in his life-time. The Exile's trauma-fuelled perspective is clearly visible in chapter 8. In Psalms of Solomon 8:7, the composer of the Psalms of Solomon clearly emphasizes the justice of God. For the psalmist, it was consistent with the nature of God and His work in history since the Creation for Him to use Gentile armies to destroy God's dwelling people and the chosen people of God. The Psalmist catalogues sins of the Jews in Psalms of Solomon 8:8-15.

      The catalogue of the sins in Psalms of Solomon 8:8-15 is a list of sins committed by the Jews that led to God's punishment of the destruction of the Jerusalem Temple, the city of Jerusalem, the nation, slaughter of the Jews by Gentile armies, and the Exile in Babylon. This is clear from Psalms of Solomon 8:16-24. Psalms of Solomon 8:16 starts by stating that it was God who brought the destroyer: "He led him from the end of the earth – the one who strikes mightily." God anointed the Babylonian King famed for his warfare to invade Jerusalem and destroy it. Psalms of Solomon 8:17 states: "He made a judgment of war against Jerusalem and her land." Psalms of Solomon 8:21 states that this foreign ruler sent by God successfully occupied the city of Jerusalem. And the reason that there was victory for the foreign army against the nation's capital was that God gave the foreign commander victory by blinding the Jews. Psalms of Solomon 8:22 states: "Because God led him with certainty amidst the blindness of them." And we see what the Babylonian conqueror and his soldiers did in the city of Jerusalem. Psalms of Solomon 8:23-24 state:

> ^{23}He exiled their rulers and every wise man in the assembly. He shed the blood of the residents of Jerusalem like waste water.
> ^{24}He led away sons and their daughters, whom they conceived in corruption.

His account accords with the deeds of King of Babylon who conquered Jerusalem and destroyed the nation. The heathen King of Babylon killed the nobles and counsellors to the king. The Gentile commander annihilated most of the population of Jerusalem. And the remainder were sent into the Exile in Babylon.

As the composer remembers what happened to Jerusalem and the people of Jerusalem by the hand of King Nebuchadnezzar, the Babylonian King who served as the servant of God in God's judgement of Israel, he blamed the Jews for what happened. Psalms of Solomon 8:25 states: "They acted according to their corruption, like their fathers." There was cultic violation. In fact, the psalmist is more specific in the following verse that the violation involved improper cultic worship in the Jerusalem Temple. Psalms of Solomon 8:26 states: "They desecrated Jerusalem and the holy things dedicated to the name of God." The two verses – Psalms of Solomon 8:25-26 – following the description of destruction of Jerusalem and the resulting Exile at the hand of the Babylonian conqueror (Psalms of Solomon 8:16-24) is, in fact, a summary of the catalogue of transgressions that led to God's judgement to bring in a foreign army in order to conquer Jerusalem and annihilate its residents. That catalogue is found in Psalms of Solomon 8:8-15.

In Psalms of Solomon 8:8-15, the catalogue of the sins of Israel that led to the complete destruction of the nation and the decimation of its populace and the Exile of a remnant are in two major catagories: (1) sexual sins of incest and adultery, and (2) cultic violation at the Jerusalem Temple. Psalms of Solomon 8:10 states that there were illicit sex relations between son and mother and between father and daughter. The next verse (Psalms of Solomon 8:11) states that there was adultery with another man's wife. These sexual sins are described in Psalms of Solomon 8:9 as sins in "worldly secrets" that angered God. Besides sexual transgressions of the populace that brought God to anger, there were violations of proper cultic worship and sacrifice that angered God. Specifically, cultic violations are listed in Psalms of Solomon 8:12-13. First in the list of cultic violations is the treating of the holy place of God as their own possession (Psalms of Solomon 8:12). In other words, Jews stole objects consecrated to God in the Jerusalem Temple and invaded a place that was reserved for worshipping God. There were objects and sacrifices that were specifically delineated for God. These were not to be touched or consumed by people. But apparently, Jews touched and consumed what should have been left alone for God. Secondly, the cultic violation involved going up to the altar of God in the state of uncleanness (Psalms of Solomon 8:13a). There were specific guidelines in the Old Testament for proper cultic worship. There were descriptions of when individuals were ritually impure, which forbade them from entering the altar of God. Apparently, these regulations were violated. Most of ritual impurity involved sex. Thus, it can be inferred that those who committed adultery were ritually impure and had no right to go up to the sanctuary. The case is the same for incest. Fathers who had sex with their daughters and mothers who had sex with their sons were ritually impure so that they were not permitted to go up to the altar. The fact that these sexual transgressors went up to the altar of

God deeply offended God. Thus, the second catalogue of cultic violations relating to the Jerusalem Temple indicates that even sexual transgression which appeared to be individual sins were linked to cultic violation and transgression of proper worship at the Jerusalem Temple.

The third cultic violation mentioned is found in Psalms of Solomon 8:13b. The third cultic violation involves polluting of the sacrifices and eating them like profane meat. Since the Jerusalem Temple cult was a cultic system built on the sacrificial system, all laws of the cult were related essentially to the sacrificial cult. Thus, it is understandable how individual sexual transgression is related to cultic violation. In the same manner, food laws – and specifically, eating of certain food – could be linked to violation of the cultic laws. It is forbidden for sacrificed meats to be consumed like profane meat. There were lambs for sacrifice and there were lambs slaughtered for popular consumption. The point is not over whether the meat is kosher or not. Rather, it is over the distinction between meat set apart for sacrifices and meat for popular consumption. Sacrificial meat, if it is not consumed according to the dictates of the law, would violate cultic laws regarding sacrificed meat. There were elaborate laws regarding how animals were to be prepared for sacrifices, how they were to be sacrificed, and how the sacrificed meat should be consumed. All these cultic aspects of the sacrificial animal/meat had to be observed for the sacrifice and the cultic practice surrounding the Jerusalem Temple to be legitimate. Consumption of sacrificed meat like profane meat was tantamount to polluting of the sacrifice. However, in Psalms of Solomon 8:13b, pollution of sacrifices should not be seen as limited to profane consumption of sacrificial meat. It was broader than that. In other words, eating of sacrificial meat as if it were profane meat is one of the ways the sacrifice could be polluted, but there were other ways as well. If the incorrect animal was offered up for sacrifice, that sacrifice could be deemed to be polluted. Furthermore, if a correct animal was not adequately prepared for the sacrifice, then the sacrifice could be ruled as polluted. The third catalogue of cultic violations must be seen as encompassing all of these types of pollution of sacrifice warned about in the Law.

All of the catalogue of transgressions is listed by the composer of the Psalms of Solomon to indicate that improper cultic practice and polluted worship at the Jerusalem Temple invalidates the physical presence of the Jerusalem Temple. In other words, form without content was meaningless. Even if the Jerusalem Temple physically stood in the chosen city of Jerusalem as the designated dwelling place of God, God could leave the place at any time due to improper worship and cultic violations. For the psalmist, the Babylonian Exile following the complete destruction of the nation happened because God chose to depart from the Jerusalem Temple and judge Jerusalem by sending in foreign armies led by a foreign commander, specifically chosen for the purpose of the destruction of the "chosen" nation and the decimation of the nation's "chosen" populace.

When the composer of the Psalms of Solomon hears the battle cry in the city of Jerusalem, he remembers what happened years before when the Babylonian army invaded and decimated the local population and destroyed the nation and sent the remnant into the Exile. Because of the collective memory of the Exile, the composer of the Psalms of Solomon beseeches God not to allow Gentiles to completely destroy the city of Jerusalem and decimate the population. The psalmist is, in effect, praying that the precedent not be repeated. Psalms of Solomon 8:36

states: "O our God, do not overlook us, lest the people consume us with none delivering." The psalmist feared destruction by the hand of Gentiles.

Psalms of Solomon 8:36, in effect, acts as the end of a "bookmark" started by Psalms of Solomon 8:1. Psalms of Solomon 8:1 relates the current experience of the composer of the Psalms of Solomon who experiences an invasion of Jerusalem by a foreign army. The description of the invasion by a foreign army continues until Psalms of Solomon 8:7, which mixes description of the invasion with the psalmist's own sentiments about the invasion. The psalmist describes himself as being afraid and his bones shaken like flax (Psalms of Solomon 8:6), and he lost his guts and his knees became weak (Psalms of Solomon 8:5) when he heard the sound of the war.

Thus, Psalms 8:1-7 actually forms the beginning of the bookmark. This book mark along with the bookmark at the other end which beseeches that Gentiles not completely destroy Jerusalem as before (Psalms of Solomon 8:36) encases the composer's description of the cataloguing of sins leading up to God's decision to destroy Jerusalem completely and decimate the population at the hand of foreign soldiers at the time of Babylonian invasion. Psalms of Solomon 8, therefore, is a piece of poetry that is self-contained that explains why proper cultic observation is essential for the viability of the Jerusalem Temple in light of the collective experience of the Exile. This beautifully encapsulated poem attests to the staying power of the Psalms of Solomon as a quintessential Late Second Temple Period document that captured the hopes and fears of Late Second Temple Period Jews.

But just as Psalms of Solomon 8 testifies to the quintessential Late Second Temple Period nature of the Psalms of Solomon as a whole in its emphasis on the remembrance of the Exile due to their transgressions, Psalms of Solomon 11 testifies to the document's quintessential Late Second Temple Period nature by approaching the Exile from an another angle; namely, that of the concept of divine ingathering. It is true that God had punished Jews and Israel for their cultic violations. It is true that the Jews were decimated and those who remained alive were exiled into far away lands, either by force or, in effect, by necessity. However, for the Jews of the Second Temple Period, it was also true that God had ingathered them back into Jerusalem by His grace and mercy. Thus, unlike the perspective of the Exile that was highly pessimistic, even though characterized by hope, the view of the Second Temple Period was from the vantage point of those who had experienced God's mercy in His act of divine ingathering. Psalms of Solomon 11 celebrates God's mercy and act of ingathering.

In this, Psalms of Solomon 11 could be seen as an encapsulation of the thanksgiving celebration of the Jews who have been restored to Jerusalem. Jews knew that God showed mercy despite the awful judgment and the Exile, so they believed that it was a part of God's nature to show mercy and ingather them. Psalms of Solomon 11 could be seen as an organized poem celebrating divine ingathering in Jerusalem.

Psalms of Solomon 11 starts in a magnificent way, with a trumpet blowing. The verse one states that this trumpet is the holy trumpet of Jubilee. Jubilee was often equated with freedom and liberty. This is logical since in the Jubilee year, slave owners were to free the slaves. In the context of Psalms of Solomon 11, the jubilee refers to the liberty of Jews from the bondage of the Exile. Psalms of Solomon 11:2 makes it clear that the freedom and liberty of the Jews were the result of God's mercy. It was

God who had freed them from the bondage of Exile. It was not human hands, even if human beings might have technically brought the process into motion for the restoration of Israel. The true reality that lay behind the visible was God's invisible hand at work. The work of divine mercy was, of course, the act of ingathering Jews to Jerusalem, the city of Zion. It is significant that both verse 1 and verse 2 mention the city by name. Jerusalem for the psalmist was the chosen city; thus, divine ingathering will have to be in Jerusalem and nowhere else. Why Jerusalem? It was because Jerusalem was the city where the House of God stood (or should stand), and this Jerusalem Temple was the dwelling place of God. The fact that the Jews were ingathered back in Jerusalem and had the Jerusalem Temple rebuilt was proof positive that God was in their midst. There were regular sacrifices and worship services in Jerusalem, and this was the proof that God had shown mercy to the Jews.

Thus, it was appropriate for the trumpet to be blown in Jerusalem and the announcement to be made that God had shown them mercy. The blow of trumpet actually was a call to worship. Since God had ingathered Jews to Jerusalem from the horrors of the Exile so that they might worship Him in His House, they should render Him worship and sacrifice that would be pleasing to Him. The trumpet call, therefore, was a call to worship of thanksgiving and sacrifice of acknowledgement regarding God's greatness and His mercy. Psalms of Solomon 11:3 clearly testifies to this understanding of the poet. The poet personifies the city of Jerusalem and bids her to behold her children being gathered in Jerusalem. In a sense, the poet claims that the city of Jerusalem itself is a witness to the ingathering of the Jews in Jerusalem as the result of God's mercy to them.

But Jerusalem as an inanimate city is not the only thing that is personified in the personification of Jerusalem in Psalms of Solomon 11. In fact, Jerusalem which is invoked in verse 3 symbolizes the residents of Jerusalem. Those Jews who have returned from the Exile could look around and see other Jews and their children gathered in Jerusalem. There were human eyewitnesses to the divine ingathering of the Jews. And they were ingathered from the East and West by God. The emphasis is clearly on God who ingathered. Psalms of Solomon 11:4 emphasizes the concept of God who ingathers. Verse 4 expands on verse 3 by providing two more locations from which God has ingathered. Whereas in verse 3, East and West are specifically mentioned as places from which God had ingathered, verse 4 states that God has ingathered from the North and from islands far away. It is interesting to note that South is missing. There are directions of East, West, and North, but instead of South, there is the designation of islands far away. It is possible that islands far away are seen as a replacement for the direction of South. There was a Jewish community in Elephantine Island in Egypt. There are papyri that survive from there. Documentary evidence seems to suggest that not only was the Jewish community in and around this island quite significant in size, but also that they were actively engaged in commerce and other types of activity in the region. This suggests that the Jewish community in this island was known to Jews of Jerusalem. And Jews from this community may have frequently visited the Jerusalem Temple. Thus, mentioning islands far away would have triggered the collective memory of Jews of Elephantine Island.

Another reason why islands far away may have replaced the direction South is that the Psalms of Solomon as a pro-Zadokite document did not want to condemn the

Zadokite Temple in Leontopolis, Egypt. Certainly, the composer of the Psalms of Solomon was pro-Zadokite. He may not have fully condoned the setting up of a competing temple in Leontopolis, but he certainly did not support the usurpation of the High Priest position by non-Zadokite priests. They were illegitimate for the position of the High Priest. And their mere occupation of the highest position in the Jerusalem Temple was problematic. In fact, Psalms of Solomon 8 is a veiled attack of the Hasmonean "desecration" of the Jerusalem Temple. Thus, while not wanting to dismiss the redemptive medium of the Jerusalem Temple, which was sacred by the virtue of God's presence in it, the poet of the Psalms of Solomon did not want to reject the legitimate priests for the office of the High Priest. Most likely, the poet harbored loyalty to the Zadokite priests in Leontopolis and a strong hope that they would be restored to the position of the High Priest – they or some other Zadokites. The important thing to note in this regard is that no one who fought for the legitimacy of the Zadokites for the position of the High Priest could dismiss any Zadokites. An errant Zadokite priest could repent and make himself worthy for the post. More likely was the possibility that the children of an errant Zadokite priest could be consecrated and prove themselves worthy to hold the office of the High Priest. Therefore, the omission of the direction South and its replacement by islands far away must be seen as strategic by the composer of the Psalms of Solomon, who is pro-Zadokite.

Although the composer of Psalms of Solomon 11 accommodates the Zadokites in Leontopolis, he is dedicated to the Jerusalem tradition of the Late Second Temple Period. In other words, the poet of Psalms of Solomon 11 believes that divine ingathering must be done in Jerusalem, ultimately. This idea is contained in the description of ingathering in verses 3 and 4. The concept of divine ingathering in Jerusalem is further emphasized in Psalms of Solomon 11:5, which accounts God's miraculous work in the process of divine ingathering. Verse 5 describes God levelling the mountains into a plain so that those being ingathered could easily walk toward their destination. The concept of God using miracles to ingather to Jerusalem can be seen as an idea drawn from the Exodus. In the Exodus, Moses, acting as God's agent, brings Israelites out of the Land of Egypt. Although Moses is the human agent in the process of ingathering of the Israelites to Jerusalem, God is always perceived as the main power behind the ingathering process. And in the Exodus and the long process of ingathering in Israel for proper cultic worship, God enacts a lot of miracles. In fact, it was with 10 plagues of Egypt that God forces the Egyptians to allow Israelites to leave Egypt. And in the wilderness, the Israelites encounter many miracles, such as God sending manna and quails for food, which are seen as a part of God's mercy and grace in ingathering Israelites to Israel for proper cultic worship. Psalms of Solomon 11:5 draws on the emphasis of God's miraculous involvement in the ingathering process.

    Besides the nature manipulation of levelling mountains to provide smooth journey, God gave those being ingathered additional miracles. According to Psalms of Solomon 11:6, God made the hills to flee before those being ingathered entered in. Furthermore, God made the woods to give Israelites shelter. God's making hills to flee can be seen as similar to levelling of the mountains, mentioned in verse 5. In both cases, God destroyed the obstacles that stood in the way of the divine ingathering. Making woods to give Jews shelter can be seen as qualitatively different from making hills flee and levelling of mountains. Whereas making hills to flee and levelling of the mountains can be seen as destructive nature manipulation in which nature is destroyed by God in one shape or form, making woods to give shelter to the Jews can be seen as a constructive nature manipulation by God. This highlights a very important point. Nature manipulation by God could be destructive or constructive, but the main purpose of the nature manipulation remains the same. Both destructive and constructive nature manipulations are meant to provide aid to those whom God ingathers. This was the case in the Exodus as well. Turning the River of Nile into blood and killing of the first born can be seen as destructive nature manipulation by God. Giving of manna and quails for food can be seen as constructive nature manipulation by God. But both of these nature manipulations had the common purpose – namely, to ingather Israelites to Israel to offer proper cultic worship to God. In the like manner, both the destructive nature manipulation of making hills to flee and constructive nature manipulation of making woods give shade had the common purpose of effectively and safely ingathering the Jews to Jerusalem.

Psalms of Solomon 11:7 continues to provide examples of nature manipulation by God to help with divine ingathering into Jerusalem. Following the second half of verse 6 where there is the positive nature manipulation of making woods give shelter, verse 7 describes the constructive nature manipulation of making trees of sweet fragrance spring up before those being ingathered. This constructive nature manipulation can be seen in the same vein as God providing food to the Israelites in the Exodus. As Israelites exited Egypt and wandered in the wilderness, headed for the Promised Land, they received manna and quail as food. God showered manna and quail from the sky, so that Israelites would not be hungry or die of hunger. God provided for the daily necessity of the Israelites in their journey toward the place where the Jerusalem Temple would ultimately be built. In the same way, God provided food by making trees of sweet fragrance sprout before the Jews as they were ingathered. This implies that God fed the Jews on their way to Jerusalem to bring proper cultic worship before God. There were miracles involved as trees sprouted up from the ground to give them fruit as food.

    But we see that the sprouting of trees had another purpose. Besides giving sweet flavored food, the miraculously sprouting trees made it possible for the Jews to travel during daytime when the sun was scorching. As many Jews had to travel through the desert, the hot mid-day sun could have discouraged their advancement during peak daylight hours. They could have tried to locate a shade and stay there for many hours until it was cool enough to travel. This would, of course, delay travel and make travel very difficult. In fact, if there were Jews who braved the afternoon sun and travelled toward the Jerusalem Temple in mid-day, many of them could die along the way. Thus, it was not merely a matter of comfort, but of necessity for life and death that there would be shade during the hot day time. By making trees sprout up, God miraculously provided the needed shade so that the Jews could travel by day, covered from the scorching mid-day sun. Because of the positive constructive nature manipulation of God, the Jews were saved from physical death. This highlights the fact that God is someone who is concerned about details. He does not merely command ingathering to Jerusalem, he guides the ingathering, taking care to meet the needs and necessities of life along the ingathering process. This is consistent with the picture of divine ingathering found in the Exodus. Israelites were headed toward the Promised Land, and they were able to travel by daytime because God guided them with a cloud. Of course, not only did the cloud provide direction to the Israelites to follow, it protected the Israelites from the dessert sun. The constructive nature manipulation was meant to save Israelites from dying of heat exhaustion and dehydration. Thus, both Exodus and Psalms of Solomon 11 share similarities in emphasizing the constructive nature manipulation by God to propel safe and efficient ingathering during the daytime. However, the Exodus accounts that God not only propelled nature manipulation during daytime but in the night time as well. God guided the Israelites during the day by clouds and in the night with the pillar of fire.

Psalms of Solomon 11:8 – the next verse – clearly shows why God effectuated nature manipulation. God worked various miracles so that the Jews would worship God in the Jerusalem Temple. The whole purpose of God's divine ingathering was so that proper cultic sacrifices and right worship would be carried out in Jerusalem. Psalms of Solomon 11:8 addresses Jerusalem, personified. What the poet-composer of Psalms of Solomon commands and demands of Jerusalem is to prepare for cultic worship. Psalms of Solomon 11:8 demands: "Put on, O Jerusalem, the garments of your glory! Prepare the robe of your holy place! For, God has spoken good for Israel into eternity and evermore." Certainly, the garment of glory refers to the fact that Jerusalem has the Jerusalem Temple where priests in holy robes conduct cultic sacrifices. In a sense, therefore, the garment of glory can be seen as analogous to the holy apparel, mentioned in the same verse. Thus, the value of Jerusalem is pointed out in Psalms of Solomon 11 as its function as the cultic center where cultic services are carried out. Since God has conducted positive nature manipulation for the Jews and ingathered them to Jerusalem, the Jews should render proper cultic worship to God. Thus, as priests put on their holy apparel and conduct proper cultic sacrifices at the Jerusalem Temple, the glory of Jerusalem shines. It is because God has been gracious and spoke favorably to Israel that the Jews should conduct proper cultic worship. The emphasis is on the priests, here, since it is the priestly group who put on holy apparel for proper cultic worship, even though the people participate in the worship service. This emphasis on the priests shows something about the poet-composer of the Psalms of Solomon. It shows that the composer of Psalms of Solomon was concerned with the priestly class and was from the priestly class. In fact, the composer was a Zadokite priest who was concerned with proper priests conducting priestly worship. There are many elements to the cultic services at the Jerusalem Temple, so the poet-composer's focus on priestly apparel cannot be seen as accidental, but strategic and intentional.

The concern with priestly clothing in Psalms of Solomon 11 can be likened to the concern of priestly clothing in the Book of Ezekiel. Because the Book of Ezekiel was written by a priest, there is a serious concern with priestly clothing. In fact, the concern with the nature, function, and apparel of priests were main concerns of priestly writings. This is not surprising. In contrast, non-priestly writings are less concerned with the priests and more concerned with forms of sacrifice or the ritual itself.

Psalms of Solomon 11, which encapsulates the whole tenor of the Psalms of Solomon as a complete document, certainly belie the priestly origin of the composition as well as its priestly concerns. This provides further evidence that the document was written by a Zadokite priest in the second century BC, rather than by a Pharisee in the first century BC, as it is commonly thought. Psalms of Solomon 11 can be seen in light of the conflict between priests – mainly between the Zadokite priests and the Hasomonean priests. The composer of the Psalms of Solomon does not belong to the group of Zadokite priests who have abandoned Jerusalem and went off to Leontopolis, Egypt, to build a competing Jewish temple to the temple in Jerusalem, "usurped" by the Hasmoneans. And the poet-composer does not belong to the group of Zadokite priests who left Jerusalem and founded an ascetic community in Qumran. The composer of the Psalms of Solomon belongs to the group of Zadokite priests who remained in Jerusalem and quietly hoped for reform and the reinstating of the Zadokite priests in the Jerusalem Temple. As the Maccabean Revolt was relatively new, he was hopeful that people would come to their senses and reinstate the Zadokite priesthood.

The fact that the Zadokite poet-composer draws attention to the priests is meant to nudge his readers to consider the importance of proper priests wearing holy robes. As he was writing when the Hasmoneans were in power, he could not make a direct attack on the Hasmoneans. Especially because the composer of the Psalms of Solomon wanted his writing to be widely distributed, he tried to draw the readers' attention to the priesthood by subtle means. The Hasmoneans in power would not block the writing or discourage wide distribution of the work of poetry because it seemed to be harmless and even laudatory on the surface level reading of the accomplishments of the Hasmoneans in purifying the Jerusalem Temple. In fact, there is everything to indicate that the Psalms of Solomon, and especially Psalms of Solomon 11, was a quintessential Late Second Temple period document that appealed to the mainstream. It is precisely in its subtle reminder to the readers of the importance of proper priesthood for proper cultic worship that the Zadokite priest writing in a difficult political situation where the Zadokites were completely disenfranchised could offer his form of resistance. It is in such a political climate that the composer of the Psalms of Solomon presents himself to be an absolute genius of his craft.

The closing of Psalms of Solomon 11 in verse 9 further shows that the poet-composer was concerned with the proper priesthood. He completely ignores the issue of proper sacrifice. This is significant in the context of Psalms of Solomon 11. This is a poem that celebrates the ingathering and restoration. In a sense, the Hasmoneans restoring the Jerusalem Temple and its cultic sacrifices was a righteous act. Now, the Jerusalemites could have daily worship and regular sacrifice. The fact of Antiochus IV Epiphanes having defiled the Jerusalem Temple is now behind them. The Jerusalem Temple is rededicated and it is a time of celebration. In this context, Psalms of Solomon 11 celebrates the restoration and languages it in terms of ingathering. Given that the poem is a celebratory one, one would expect a note of joy over the fact that proper sacrifices are restored. Sacrifice is a concern of the poet-composer. We know this from other parts of Psalms of Solomon which criticize desecration of the sacrifices, such as Psalms of Solomon 8. Thus, it is peculiar that proper sacrifices are not mentioned in Psalms of Solomon 11, explicitly. But this is intentional, and this highlights the main point of the Zadokite poet-composer regarding proper cultic sacrifice: proper priesthood is important. In other words, proper priests should be the ones bringing glory to the Jerusalem Temple. And, of course, for the poet-composer, the Zadokites were the legitimate, proper priests.

In this vein, when the poet-composer states in Psalms of Solomon 11:9 – "May the LORD do what he has promised concerning Israel and in Jerusalem!" – he is not merely uttering a blessing. In fact, this could be seen as a warning, or even a curse formula. In effect, this is meant to warn his readers that God could destroy Jerusalem and Israel as He has before. When the Jews were decimated by the Babylonians with an unbeliever King Nebuchadnezzar at the helm, they were under the covenant with God. In the same manner, the Jews who are under the mercy of God's covenant now could receive serious blow from God if they are not careful to observe proper cultic worship. As the verse immediately preceding emphasized the importance of the holy priesthood, the readers are reminded of their cultic observations to God in this area as well. There were priests who were to guide the services of the Jerusalem Temple. Proper High Priest was a Zadokite one. Currently, there was a Hasmonean occupying the seat of the High Priest. This was an aberration.

Thus, the readers are cautioned and even warned. Yes, the covenant is in effect, but then, the covenant was in effect when God used a foreign army to completely destroy the Jerusalem Temple, decimate the Jewish population, and dismantle Israel as a nation. Although the Jews might have escaped destruction at Antiochus IV Epiphanes' hands, they are not clear and free. That might have been a warning to the Jews. True destruction could be on its way. And this time, if they do not take care to observe the proper cultic worship at the Jerusalem Temple, including the value of proper priests, they could experience decimation and destruction.

In this vein, what the LORD spoke concerning Israel and Jerusalem could be seen as a reminder of the prophetic warnings against Jerusalem and Israel in many of the Old Testament's prophetic books. To who did God speak? God spoke through His prophets. What did God's prophets prophesy? They prophesied the words of God that Israel would be destroyed and Jerusalem decimated. This explains the concluding part of Psalms of Solomon 11:9: "May the LORD raise up Israel in the name of his glory! The mercy of the LORD is upon Israel for eternity and evermore."

The important emphasis is on God's glory. The Zadokite poet-composer beseeches that Israel be lifted up in the name of God's glory. He does not want Israel to be lifted up for its own sake or the sake of the Jews. Israel should be lifted up to glorify God. Of course, the understanding is that Israel could be – and even, should be – destroyed for the sake of God's glory. In other words, if Israel does not offer proper cultic worship to God and does not glorify God, it is only right and just that God destroy Jerusalem for the sake of His glory. This is consistent with the teaching of the Old Testament, both in the prophetic portions and in historical writings.

The composer of Psalms of Solomon shows himself to be remarkably consistent with the Old Testament. In fact, his position was the normative position in the Late Second Temple period. The Jews of the Second Temple period knew that the First Jerusalem Temple was destroyed when the covenant of God was still in effect because they were remiss in offering proper cultic worship to God. The Old Testament describes that the destruction of Jerusalem brought glory to God. In fact, it was for the glory of God's name that Jerusalem was destroyed, Jerusalemites annihilated, and the country of Israel dismantled. The poet-composer's invocation of God's name and His glory is a warning because Second Temple Jews knew what God did to them to protect the glory of His name. The poet sides with God and His right to annihilate the Jews and destroy Jerusalem for the glory of His name. This is understood when the poet emphasizes the glory of God's name and the raising up of Israel just for the sake of God's name.

Similarly, the final line of Psalms of Solomon, calling for the mercy of God on Israel can be seen as a warning, rather than a blessing. It is akin to someone in America saying to someone in closing: "May God have mercy on your soul." He is not saying a blessing; rather, he is sealing his fate. A person will say this to someone who is going to a sure death. There is no hope for that person to survive a war or a certain ordeal, so the final greeting is for mercy on his soul after his death. The person uttering the greeting (or curse) is not actually saying that he wants God to have mercy on his soul. He is basically saying, "It's tough for you. You are going to die." It's a euphemistic way of saying "you are going to die." In the same way, the final formula of seeming blessing is actually a warning or a curse. May God have mercy on Israel. The poet-composer would not say this if he felt that the Jews were facing many days of joy and happiness. He is saying it because he anticipates difficult days ahead. He thinks that the Jews will encounter many difficulties. And in fact, he believes that God will destroy the Jews in a catastrophic judgement. Otherwise, he would not end the poem with an euphemistic saying of certain death. This dire warning is consistent with the fact that the poet-composer is a Zadokite priest who sees destruction of Jews and of Israel in the years ahead because they have placed Hasmoneans in the office of the High Priest, against cultic norms. In fact, he is reminding his readers of the judgement from this cultic violation. Yes, the Jews may be celebrating victory over Antiochus IV Epiphanes, but it is pre-mature because worse days are ahead. So, may God have mercy on you.

Psalms of Solomon 11 shows itself to be a quintessential Late Second Temple Period document. It shares the concerns of all Late Second Temple Period documents regarding proper cultic worship and observance. And in a sense, Psalms of Solomon 11 is an encapsulation of the whole of the Psalms of Solomon, which as a whole is a quintessential Late Second Temple Period document. Psalms of Solomon as a whole is concerned with proper cultic worship. It is a collection of poems that details various cultic violations, reminds what happened in the First Temple Period when the proper cultic worship is violated, and warns of what could happen if careful attention to details is missing.

However, although the Psalms of Solomon is a quintessential Late Second Temple Period document sharing the concerns of this time with proper cultic worship and observance, it is distinctive as a pro-Zadokite document. The Psalms of Solomon reflects the emphasis that the proper cultic worship in the Jerusalem Temple requires proper priests and a Zadokite as the High Priest. In the state where Zadokite priests were disenfranchised and those who are Zadokites walk under Hasmonean shadows, the poet-composer who is a Zadokite priest himself writes in a subtle way to protect himself while in his own way protesting the current situation. While it is important to recognize the quintessential Late Second Temple Period nature of the Psalms of Solomon, it is important also to emphasize the distinctive pro-Zadokite emphasis of the Psalms of Solomon.

Chapter Four: The Covenant

The Psalms of Solomon is a quintessential Late Second Temple Period document. Despite the anti-Hasmonean and pre-Maccabean propaganda, the Psalms of Solomon is a part of the ethos of the Late Second Temple Period. In fact, the issue was over specific details and not about the general principle. The most important principle was that the Jerusalem Temple is the central redemptive medium and represented the fulfilment of God's covenant. The Zadokites believed that their presence was integral to the correct operation of the Jerusalem Temple and the Hasmoneans did not. But both the Zadokites and the Hasmoneans believed that the Jerusalem Temple was a central redemption medium and the fulfilment of the covenantal promise of God. In fact, the covenant concept was what undergirded the power of the Jerusalem Temple. Thus, the covenant was a central theme dominating in Late Second Temple literature and thought.

As a central concept attached to the Jerusalem Temple, the covenant concept deserves some attention. What is the covenant and how did it play a central role in popping up the Jerusalem tradition of the Late Second Temple Period? No discussion of the covenant can exist without the discussion of the Abrahamic covenant as found in the book of Genesis. The covenant with Abraham is found in Genesis 15 and in Genesis 17.

A main question attached to the Abrahamic covenant has been whether the covenant was unilateral or bilateral. In other words, were there requirements for both parties of the covenant? Surprisingly, there have been scholars who have argued that the covenant between

Abraham and God was unilateral and not bilateral. These scholars have argued that God had promised to Abraham certain blessings of the covenant regardless of what Abraham (and his descendants) did. These scholars argued that the covenant was a promise of God to Abraham and his descendants certain blessings and not a system of reward and punishment based on the fulfilment of stipulations of the covenant by Abraham and Abraham's descendants.

Although this position has enjoyed consensus among some scholars and in some settings – even highly academic environments – this position is seriously flawed and must be discarded. There are several strong arguments for why the argument for the unilateral nature of the covenant must be discarded. They can be identified under the categories of (1) the nature of covenants, (2) textual evidence, (3) historical and historiographical evidence.

First, let us discuss the nature of covenants. It is simply wrong to equate a covenant with a unilateral promise. Covenant, by nature, is an agreement between two parties. A document cannot be called a covenant if it did not require obligations from both of the contracting parties. The covenant, therefore, is a contract with stipulations for observance by both parties. And the covenant releases either of the parties from the covenant in the event of covenant violation by the other party. In fact, in most cases, like as in the nature of the covenants, the violation of the contractual obligation requires a reparation or penalty. The word ברית is not used in an accidental way. In fact, ברית is intentional and emphasizes the contractual obligations of both parties. For anyone – even a scholar – to ignore the name ברית applied to the covenant between Abraham and God and argue for a unilateral promise is not only dishonest but also flatly wrong. A contract is not a contract if there are not stipulations for both parties. In the same way, ברית is not a ברית is there are not stipulations for both parties. When God made a covenant with Abraham, there were stipulations for both God and for Abraham.

What were the covenant stipulations? God's contractual obligation was to give Abraham land and make him and his descendants into a great nation. Abraham's contractual obligation was to circumcise every male in his house and in his business, employed by him. Either of the contracting parties could break their contractual obligation if the other party failed to keep their contractual obligation. Thus, if Abraham and his descendants did not circumcise all of the males in his family and his business, then God could refuse to give land to Abraham and his descendants and refuse to make Abraham and his descendants into a great nation.

Ancillary to these main stipulations was the stipulation that God would be the God of Abraham and his descendants if Abraham and his descendants lived in the Promised Land. If Abraham and his descendants lived outside of the Promised Land, then God was free from this obligation to be the God of Abraham and his descendants. In other words, if Jews lived in the Diaspora, God – under the stipulation of the covenant – could refuse to be their God and to recognize them as His people. The very act of living outside of Israel meant that the covenant was broken and Jews were no longer protected by God.

The textual evidence strongly supports the nature of the bilateral agreement of the Abrahamic covenant. In Genesis 15, God tells Abraham to cut pieces of the animal. This is a signature of Abraham signing on the dotted line to give the right to God to execute him and his descendants if they broke the covenant. Thus, the covenant was sealed with the retributive reparation clause for the breaking of the contract by Abraham and his descendants. God was given the right to annihilate Jews by whichever means He saw fit.

God also passed through the cut pieces of the animal. This was God's way of signing the contract. If God did not keep his contractual agreement, then Abraham and his descendants could "kill" God. Thus, contractual violation by either party required death of the party breaking the contract.

Genesis 17 also affirms this bilateral nature of the covenant for the contracting parties in the Abrahamic covenant. Genesis 17 clearly stipulates that God would give Abraham and his descendants the Promised Land if Abraham kept his covenantal obligation of circumcision and cultic observance. If Abraham and his descendants broke the covenantal obligation, then the covenantal requirement for God to give land was abrogated. In fact, the covenanted stipulation was not merely for the time period before the land was given by God since the covenant was a ברית עולם. It was an everlasting covenant. What this means is that if at any point after God gives the land to an everlasting point in timeline (eternity), if Abraham and his descendants broke their covenantal stipulation, then the land which they already possessed (as the result of God's fulfilled covenantal obligation) could be taken away by God. Thus, the land was never fully secure in Jewish hands. At any moment that they violated their covenantal stipulations, they lost both their right to land (before possession) and their ownership of land (after possession).

In a sense, Genesis 15 could be seen as a more aggressive negative description of the consequences of the covenant breaking – death for the breaking party – than Genesis 17, which focuses on the promises of God in the event of covenant keeping. However, it must be emphasized that both Genesis 15 and Genesis 17 presume the bilateral nature of covenant relations. God will bless Abraham and his descendants only if they keep their part of the covenant, such as living in Israel and circumcising their children. In the event that they broke the covenant by living outside of Israel or not circumcising their children, God would punish them by the curses of the covenant, which would be death.

The bilateral nature of the Abrahamic covenant and its stipulations is confirmed in other texts of the Old Testament. Both the pre-exilic texts and exilic texts confirm the bilateral nature of the Abrahamic covenant.

Among the pre-exilic texts is the dominance of pre-exilic prophetic writings that support the concept of bilateral agreement of the covenant. The covenant made with Abraham and his descendants was not unilateral in nature; rather, the covenant required fulfillment of obligations by both of the parties of the covenant. Thus, if the descendants of Abraham (represented in the people of Israel) did not observe the covenant, then God could take punitive measures against them, whose stipulation is built into the covenant itself. The punitive measures are described as "the curses of the covenant." The pre-exilic prophets warn both the king of Israel and the Israel's populace of the impending "curses of the covenant." In a sense, these pre-exilic prophets were prosecutors of God bringing a charge against the king of Israel and the Israelite people. The charge, of course, was that they had broken the covenant with God. Therefore, the judgement was that they must suffer the consequences or the curses of the covenant.

The pre-exilic prophets are specific in their accusation against the king and the people of how they broke the covenant. The king broke the covenant in not enforcing proper cultic observance and worship. The prophets of God blamed the king for the state of affairs of the country. The country had, in effect, become atheist because the king refused to legislate proper worship of God. In effect, the king is blamed for tolerating idolatry that has swept through the land. It was the obligation of the king to use his political, military, and economic power (of the state) to protect and encourage proper cultic worship of God. But the king focused on all other matters except for the proper worship of God. Thus, the prophet was accusing the king of fulfilling his covenantal obligations and emphasized that God will punish him for this. Of course, the punishment of God involved the destruction of his kingdom. God will destroy the country which has gone in the wrong direction because the ruler failed to fulfil his obligations to God.

But pre-exilic prophets do not merely bring charges against the king. The prosecutors of God bring charges against the people of Israel. The pre-exilic prophets accuse the people of breaking the covenant with God. Their violation was not engaging in proper cultic observance as was mandated by the covenant with God. Thus, people have participated in worship of idols and sexual debauchery associated with idol worship. Thus, the prophets of God accuse them of prostituting themselves before idols. Some prophets are specific in pointing out that even those who might have been circumcised, in effect, broke even that covenantal stipulation "in spirit." They argue that although they were circumcised in their flesh, they were not circumcised in their hearts. The pre-exilic prophets were relentless in emphasizing the fact of covenant breaking by the people of Israel. Of course, the breaking of the covenant by the people of Israel meant that God no longer had to keep His covenantal stipulation. Thus, the right to land was gone as well as the possession of the land. The prophets claimed that because the people violated the covenant, God would take away the land of Israel from them. The curses of the covenant would be meted out to them by God. God will not only take away their land according to the curses of the covenant, God will annihilate a large number of them and exile the remnant into distant lands. The threat of the pre-exilic prophets against the people of Israel and the Israelite king was very real and imminent.

Of course, by the exilic period, the curses of the covenant were realized. Therefore, exilic prophets writing explain the fact of the realization of the curses of the covenant. The exilic prophets explain primarily the question of why God had taken the land of Israel away from the Jews and allowed so many of them to be slaughtered at the hand of the Gentiles. Interestingly enough, the brunt of the blame for Jewish death is blamed on the Jews themselves. It was because the Jews failed to observe their covenantal obligations that God slaughtered them and brought the curses of the covenant to fruition.

The exilic prophets are interested primarily in exonerating God from any blame for the genocide of the Jews at the hand of Gentiles. Thus, the Old Testament is littered with statements that the Jews got what they deserved in their genocide. They were not victims; rather, the Jews received a just punishment from God for violating the covenantal agreement. It was right for God to slaughter the Jews, and it was right for the Jews to be slaughtered. Furthermore, it was righteous for God to use Gentiles to slaughter the Jews in divine judgment. In fact, the exilic prophets refer to the Gentiles who carry out genocide against the Jews as God's anointed servants. It was God Himself who chose these Gentiles to render to God service and bring judgment to the Jews by slaughtering them. Why was this righteous? It was the curses of the covenant that was reserved for the violators of the covenant.

It is important to see that there is consistency in the understanding of the covenant as the binding bilateral contract within the whole gamut of the Old Testament. From the documents describing the covenant-making to the explanation of why God chose to bring about the genocide of the Jews, the Old Testament writers consistently point to the bilateral nature of the covenant and Jews' contractual obligation. Should the Jews violate the contract, Jews would have to be annihilated as per covenantal stipulation.

This attitude persists in the post-exilic period as well. The emphasis of the exilic period was passed down to the lowest common denominator in the Israelite society. It was righteous for God to slaughter the Jews and send the remnant into exile, and it would still be righteous for God to slaughter the Jews and send the remnant into exile. This was the fundamental worldview of the post-exilic period. They assumed that the covenant was bilateral and that the Jews are required to observe their contractual obligations. The Second Temple Period writers and populace were aware that breaking their contractual stipulations would result in God's retaliatory response (or the clauses of the covenant) that could include complete destruction of the land and the genocide of the most of the populace.

This understanding of the bilateral nature of the covenant with God both informs and sustains the main flow of the literature from the Second Temple Period, even many years after the end of the exile. Thus, it is not surprising to find a strong emphasis in the Second Temple Period about proper cultic observance at the Jerusalem Temple.

Psalms of Solomon

The Jerusalem Temple was the physical manifestation of God's keeping of His covenantal stipulation. It was, therefore, an important reminder to the Jews that they must fulfil their covenantal stipulation to God. If they failed in this regard, then the curses of the covenant would apply and the Jerusalem Temple could again be destroyed. Of course, such curses of the covenant would be accompanied by the genocide of the populace and complete destruction of the country.

Late Second Temple Period writers were consistent with these writings from the earlier part of the post-exilic period in emphasizing the bilateral nature of the covenant with God. But unlike them, the Late Second Temple Period writers used the covenant concept strategically and propagandistically in the context of intra-Jewish conflict. Unlike the earlier post-exilic period and the earlier part of the Second Temple Period, the Late Second Temple Period experienced fragmentation of Jews into Jewish sectarianism. And they all vied for power centered around the Jerusalem Temple. Thus, it is not surprising how the covenant concept came to be used propagandistically by Jews against other Jews. If a group of Jews unrighteously usurped the power of the Jerusalem Temple and violated the covenant, God could bring the curses down on Jerusalem and destroy the city and the temple. Once the curses of the covenant were directed at Jerusalem by God, all would suffer. Thus, various Jewish sectarian groups argued that it was better to have a violent civil war and kill the offending Jews in order to save the city, the temple, and the majority of the people. It is in this context and outlook, the poet of the Psalms of Solomon composed his pro-Zadokite propaganda. The Zadokite composer reminded his Jewish audience that God had annihilated Jews and destroyed Jerusalem before and that He could do it again, since the Hasmoneans had usurped the high priest position of the Jerusalem Temple that legitimately belonged to the Zadokites and also the king position that legitimately belonged to descendants of King David. Covenant stipulations for proper cultic worship was not being observed and, thus, God could pursue the curses of the covenant against Jews of Jerusalem. This worldview of the Zadokite poet-composer is consistent with the worldview found in the Old Testament among pre-exilic, exilic, and post-exilic prophets regarding the covenant.

No discussion of the covenant in the Late Second Temple Period would be complete without a discussion of the covenant concept in the New Testament. The most prominent and the most influential New Testament scholar writing about the covenant (as perceived by the early Christians) is Professor E. P. Sanders of Duke University.

Professor E. P. Sanders bases his arguments about the covenant concept of early Christianity primarily on the writings of St. Paul – especially, through his discussion of the Book of Galatians. Sanders argues that the covenant concept in the Book of Galatians represented the dominant position of early Christianity and is consistent with other books of the New Testament, by in large. Thus, Sanders uses the Book of Galatians as the quintessential New Testament text on the early Christian understanding of the covenant concept.

In his writings, Professor E. P. Sanders emphasizes a principle called *covenantal nomism*. He states that Paul argued for the principle that one goes into the covenant by grace, but one stays in by the works of the law. Thus, if those who are allowed into the covenant community are not rigorous in their observation of the law, then they would be cast out of the covenant. In other words, God allowed people into the covenant by grace but there were stipulations that the people had to observe to stay in the covenant community.

It is clear to see that E. P. Sanders sees continuity in the covenant concept from the Late Second Temple Period. As discussed, it was assumed that God made a covenant with Abraham and his descendants, but this covenant was a bilateral contract with requirements for the contracting parties. The obligations of Abraham and his descendants focused on cultic purity and proper worship of God. When Abraham and his descendants violated the contract, then God was not obligated to keep his part of the covenant. Thus, the curses of the covenant would apply. The descendants of Abraham breaking the contract via cultic violation would be expelled from the covenant or receive the curses of the covenant. The covenant was made between God and Abraham (and his descendants) by grace of God but the descendants of Abraham could only stay in the covenant if they fulfilled their covenantal obligation. Thus, when the Israelites violated the covenant, God destroyed the Jerusalem Temple, annihilated the Jews of Jerusalem, and obliterated the country. The remnant who survived the genocide wrought by God (through divinely designated human agents) for the breaking of the contractual agreement by the Jews was sent away into the exile in Babylon.

The Late Second Temple Period writers assumed this principle to be true. It was by God's grace that they were a part of the covenant with God. But in order to stay in the covenant, they had to keep their contractual obligations. Failure to observe their contractual obligation would result in God suing them on the penalty clause of the contract. This idea permeates the literature of the Late Second Temple Period and could be seen as the defining principle among the Jews of the Late Second Temple Period.

Thus, it seems logical why E. P. Sanders would describe the dominant notion of the covenant in the person of Paul, who after all was a Pharisee before his conversion to Christianity, as being connected to the dominant Jewish understanding of God's covenant, current in the Late Second Temple period and even after the destruction of the Jerusalem Temple at the hand of the Romans in 70 AD and the Roman annihilation of Jews in Jerusalem.

However, not all scholars agree that E. P. Sanders is correct in his argument that the early Christians viewed the covenant in the way construed through the flow of Late Second Temple Period Judaism. Professor James Dunn of Durham University is a central opponent of the *covenant nomism* concept of Professor E. P. Sanders.

Professor James Dunn states that Paul argued for inclusion in the covenant through grace *and* staying in the covenant through grace. In a sense, Dunn is emphasizing the divergence of Christianity from the dominant Jewish position of the period in the conceptualization of the covenant concept. This point becomes clear when one reads other books by Dunn discussing the question of the separation between Judaism and Christianity. Dunn argues that the parting of the ways between Judaism and Christianity was quite early. In fact, he dates it to a period when the New Testament documents were still being written (at least, he describes the fracture as having started then). The divergence in the covenant concept, of course, points to the early break between the followers of Jesus of Nazareth and the followers of Judaism.

E. P. Sanders, based on his thesis, argued that the break came much later. In fact, Sanders dates the break between Judaism and Christianity about 100 years after the date given by James Dunn. Sanders does not see Christianity as a part of normative Judaism, but he argues for a greater flow of Jews between Jewish religious settings and Christian religious settings. Of course, this would not really have been an issue for Gentiles who converted to Christianity. Most Gentile converts to Christianity did not have any Jewish settings to which they were tied. If anything, they had to struggle to pull themselves away from Pagan settings. So, the issue of "the break" between Judaism and Christianity as construed and discussed by Sanders is quite irrelevant for most of the early Christians. From the very beginning, the number of Gentile Christians outnumbered the number of Christians who converted to Judaism.

More importantly, New Testament texts tend to support Dunn's explication of the early Christian understanding of the covenant rather than Sanders' covenantal nomism. For instance, the Gospel of John emphasizes that those who become part of the covenant are those who believe in Jesus of Nazareth. Of course, faith or belief is distinguished from action. One could argue that faith can lead to works but she cannot equate faith and works as one and the same. When one says that faith leads to works, one is arguing for causality. Faith causes works. Thus, when the Gospel of John argues that one becomes a part of the covenant, one does so through faith. Of course, faith on the part of humans implies grace on the part of God. It is by God's grace that without any action or human work, they are received as a part of the covenant.

The Gospel of John does not merely state that one gets in by grace. The Gospel of John argues that one stays in by faith or by grace. The whole Gospel of John can be an explication of the importance of faith in Jesus Christ as a means to be saved and stay saved. The Gospel of John is certainly more consistent with James Dunn's construal of the early Christian understanding of the covenant rather than the covenant nomism position of E. P. Sanders.

    This is not only the case with the Gospel of John. The Synoptic Gospels support James Dunn's explication of the early Christian understanding of the covenant rather than the explanation offered by E. P. Sanders. There are many factors that testify to the concept of "getting in" and "staying in" by grace. Perhaps, the best example of it is found in the concept of the calling of the 12 apostles. Obviously, it was by God's grace that the 12 apostles were called. They did not do anything to deserve being called as apostles. Jesus of Nazareth walked along the bank of Galilee and randomly called those who were there to be his disciples. We see that these disciples who "got in" also "stayed in" by grace. None of the disciples were kicked out of the "covenant." Even when St. Peter denied Jesus Christ three times – an act that amounts to betrayal of God in early Christianity – Jesus Christ did not kick him out of the covenant. In fact, St. Peter was made into the first "pope." When St. Thomas doubted Jesus Christ's resurrection, Jesus of Nazareth did not kick him out of the covenant; rather, Jesus of Nazareth showed Thomas his nail-pierced hands and feet. St. Thomas "got in" through grace, and he "stayed in" by grace. This was even the case with Judas Iscariot. Judas Iscariot "got in" by grace into the covenant and became Jesus' disciple. Even after Judas Iscariot took 30 pieces of silver from the Jews to betray Jesus Christ, he – knowing what Judas Iscariot did – did not kick him out of the covenant. Jesus of Nazareth merely said that it would have been better had he not been born. Indeed, Judas Iscariot "got in" by grace, and he "stayed in" by grace. The Gospel account tells us that Judas Iscariot left the covenant by his own will when he decided to commit suicide. This, in essence, affirms the principle that you get into the covenant by grace and you stay in by grace. Of course, you can always leave the covenant on your own accord.

It is not only in the Gospels that James Dunn's idea of "getting in" and "staying in" by grace is upheld and E. P. Sanders' position proved to be wrong. In much of the Pauline epistles, the covenant is understood to be that in which one gets in by grace and one stays in by grace. In this, early Christian understanding of the covenant shows itself to be completely different from the understanding of Late Second Temple Judaism.

Paul's emphasis on "getting in" and "staying in" focuses on grace. Even in the Book of Romans, the concept of election is outlined in terms of grace. By grace, there is predestination. And those who are predestined are effectually called, and those who are effectively called are justified as righteous by God. And those who are justified will be sanctified. And those who are sanctified will be glorified. There is the emphasis in Romans that God guides the whole process. For instance, the verse that He began a good work in you will complete it shows that those who "get in" by grace will "stay in" by grace.

For the early Christians, the covenant was not understood in terms of the way that Jews of the Late Second Temple Period understood it. For the early Christians, the covenant has been fulfilled in the person and work of Jesus Christ. Thus, it was through faith in Christ that they could be a part of the New Covenant and it was through faith that they could stay in the New Covenant. One "gets in" by grace, and one "stays in" by grace.

The early Christian understanding of the covenant and their conscious rejection of the predominant Late Second Temple Period Jewish understanding of the covenant highlighted the conflict between Jews and converts to Christ from the very early stage. It is no accident that the Gospel describes Jesus of Nazareth in conflict not only with all of the Jewish groups of his time but also with the Jerusalem Temple itself. Jesus Christ is described as storming the Jerusalem Temple and disturbing the peace. Jesus inflicted wilful destruction of property and visibly (and clearly) registered his opposition with the institution of the Jerusalem Temple. He offended all the Jews by calling the Jerusalem Temple his father's house and accusing that it had become "a den of robbers." And Jesus of Nazareth claimed that the Jerusalem Temple should be a house of prayer. It is important to recognize that the Jerusalem Temple was not primarily a house of prayer for the Jews. The Jerusalem Temple was primarily a place for atonement and sacrifice. What Jesus was doing in his criminal disturbance of the Jerusalem Temple was to oppose the very existence of the Jerusalem Temple's sacrificial cult. In essence, Jesus of Nazareth was rejecting the Jerusalem Temple as an institution of cultic worth.

In this regard, Jesus of Nazareth clearly set himself against the Jews of the Late Second Temple Period. The Jews of the Late Second Temple Period disagreed about who should be leaders in the Jerusalem Temple. Some supported the Hasmoneans and others the Zadokites; however, none would have stated that the Jerusalem Temple was unnecessary as a place of cultic sacrifice to God. The Jerusalem Temple existed as the House of God for Him to receive sacrifices and cultic worship. This point was agreed on by all Jews, whatever their particular persuasion or political position. This is quite understandable since the Jerusalem Temple represented the presence of God in the Promised Land and the fulfilment of the covenant. It was indeed an affirmation of the covenant made between God and Abraham and his descendants in the minds of Late Second Temple Period Jews.

The New Testament conceptualization of the covenant, or the New Covenant, works to show the Psalms of Solomon as an essential part of dominant Jewish thinking of the Late Second Temple Period and its understanding of the covenant as quintessentially Jewish. The difference explains why Jews organized to kill the early Christians. Jesus of Nazareth attacked the central symbol of Judaism for all Jews – the Jerusalem Temple. And this same Jesus and his followers attacked the central concept attached to the Jerusalem Temple – namely, the covenant with Abraham and his descendants.

Bibliography

Aberbach, Moses. "Historical Allusions of Chapter IV, XI, and XIII of the Psalms of Solomon." *Jewish Quarterly Review* 41 (1951) 379-396.

Abrahams, I. "The Psalms of Solomon." *Jewish Quarterly Review* 9 (1897) 539-549.

Atkinson, Kenneth. *An Intertextual Study of the Psalms of Solomon.* Lewiston: Mellen, 2001.

Atkinson, Kenneth. *I Cried to the Lord: A Study of the Psalms of Solomon's Historical Background and Social Setting.* Leiden: Brill, 2004.

Baars, Willem. "A New Fragment of the Greek Version of the Psalms of Solomon." *Vetus Testamentum* 11 (1961) 441-444.

Begrich, Joachim. "Der Text der Psalmen Salomos." *Zeitschrift für die neutestamentliche Wissenschaft* 38 (1939) 131-164.

Berrin, Shani. "Pesher Nahum, Psalms of Solomon and Pompey." *Reworking the Bible: Apocryphal and Related Texts at Qumran.* Edited by Esther G. Chazon. Leiden: Brill, 2005. Pages 65-84.

Bibliography

Brock, Sebastian P. "Psalms of Solomon." *The Apocryphal Old Testament*. Edited by H. F. D. Sparks. Oxford: Clarendon, 1984. Pages 649-682.

Charlesworth, James H. (Editor). *The Bible and the Dead Sea Scrolls: The Second Princeton Symposium on Judaism and Christian Origins*. Waco: Baylor University Press, 2006.

Charlesworth, James H. (Editor). *The Old Testament Pseudepigrapha*. Garden City: Doubleday, 1983-1985.

Charlesworth, James H. *The Old Testament Pseudepigrapha and the New Testament: Prolegomena for the Study of Christian Origins*. Cambridge: Cambridge University Press, 1985.

Charlesworth, James H. *The Pseudepigrapha and Modern Research with a Supplement*. Chico: Scholars Press, 1981.

Charlesworth, James H. (Editor). *Qumran-Messianism: Studies on the Messianic Expectations in the Dead Sea Scrolls*. Tübingen: Mohr/Siebeck, 1998.

Davenport, Gene L. "The 'Anointed of the Lord' in Psalms of Solomon 17." *Ideal Figures in Ancient Judaism: Profiles and Paradigms*. Edited by George W. E. Nickelsburg and John J. Collins. Chico: Scholars Press, 1980.

De Jonge, Marinus. *De Toekomstverwachting in Psalmen van Salomo*. Leiden: Brill, 1965.

De Jonge, Marinus. *Jewish Eschatology, Early Christian Christology, and the Testament of the Twelve Patriarchs.* Leiden: Brill, 1991.

De Jonge, Marinus. *Pseudepigrapha of the Old Testament as Part of Christian Literature: The Case of the Testament of the Twelve Patriarchs and the Greek Life of Adam and Eve.* Leiden: Brill, 2003.

De Jonge, Marinus. "The Psalms of Solomon." *Outside the Old Testament.* Edited by Marinus de Jonge. Cambridge: Cambridge University Press, 1985. Pages 159-177.

De Jonge, Marinus. *The Testament of the Twelve Patriarchs: A Critical Edition of the Greek Text.* Leiden: Brill, 1978.

Dimant, Devorah. "A Cultic Term in the Psalms of Solomon in the Light of the Septuagint." *Textus* 9 (1981) 28-51. In Modern Hebrew.

Efron, Joshua. "The Psalms of Solomon, the Hasmonean Decline and Christianity." *Zion* 9 (1981) 28-51. In Modern Hebrew.

Embry, Brad. "The *Psalms of Solomon* and the New Testament: Intertextuality and the Need for a Re-Evaluation." *Journal for the Study of the Pseudepigrapha* 13 (2002) 99-136.

Frankenberg, W. *Die Datierung der Psalmen Salomos: Ein Beitrag zur jüdischen Geschichte.* Giessen: Ricker, 1896.

Bibliography

Franklyn, P. N. "The Cultic and Pious Climax of Eschatology in the Psalms of Solomon." *Journal for the Study of Judaism* 18 (1987) 1-17.

Gray, G. Buchanan. "Psalms of Solomon." *The Apocrypha and Pseudepigrapha of the Old Testament in English (Volume 2)*. Edited by R. H. Charles. Oxford: Clarendon, 1913. Pages 625-652.

Hann, Robert R. *The Manuscript History of the Psalms of Solomon*. Chico: Scholars Press, 1982.

Harris, Rendel. *The Odes and Psalms of Solomon*. Cambridge: Cambridge University Press, 1911.

Harris, J. Rendel, and Alphonse Mingana. *The Odes and Psalms of Solomon* Manchester: Manchester University Press, 1916, 1920.

Holm-Nielsen, Svend. *Die Psalmen Salomos*. Gütersloh: Mohn, 1977.

Kaiser, Otto. "Beobachtungen zur Komposition und Redaktion der Psalmen Salomos." *Das Manna fällt auch heute noch: Beiträge zur Geschichte und Theologie des Alten, Ersten Testaments – Festschrift für Erich Zenger*. Edited by Frank-Lothar Hossfeld and Ludger Schwienhorst-Schönberger. Freiburg: Herder, 2004. Pages 362-378.

Kim, Heerak Christian. "An Apology for God: Psalms of Solomon 11 and Its Jerusalem Tradition." *Hebrew, Jewish and Early Christian Studies: Academic Es-*

says. Edited by Heerak Christian Kim. Cheltenham: The Hermit Kingdom Press, 2005. Pages 1-29.

Kim, Heerak Christian. *Key Signifier as Literary Device: Its Definition and Function in Literature and Media.* Lewiston: Mellen, 2006.

Kim, Heerak Christian. *The Jerusalem Tradition in the Late Second Temple Period: Diachronic and Synchronic Developments Surrounding Psalms of Solomon 11.* Lanham: University Press of America, 2007.

Kuhn, Karl Georg. *Die älteste Textgestalt der Psalmen Salomos.* Stuttgart: Kohlhammer, 1937.

Lana, Maurizio. "Salmi di Salomone." *Apocrifi dell'Antico Testamento.* Edited by Paolo Sacchi. Brescia: Paideia, 1989. Pages 39-146.

Nickelsburg, George W. E. "The Psalms of Solomon." *Jewish Literature between the Bible and Mishnah: A Historical and Literary Introduction.* Minneapolis: Fortress, 2005. Pages 238-247.

Perles, Felix. *Zur Erklärung der Psalmen Salomos.* Berlin: Peiser, 1911.

Rahlfs, Alfred. "Psalmi Salomonis." *Septuaginta (Volume 2).* Stuttgart: Deutsche Bibelgesellschaft, 1979. Pages 471-489.

Schüpphaus, Joachim. *Die Psalmen Salomos: Ein Zeugnis Jerusalmer Theologie und Frömmigkeit in der Mitte*

Bibliography

des vorchristlichen Jahrhunderts. Leiden: Brill, 1977.

Tromp, Johannes. "The Sinners and the Lawless in Psalm of Solomon 17." *Novum Testamentum* 35 (1993) 344-361.

Viteau, J. *Les Psaumes de Salomon: Introduction, Texte Grec et Traduction.* Paris : Letouzey et Ané, 1911.

Wright, Robert B. "The Psalms of Solomon, the Pharisees and the Essenes." *1972 Proceedings: International Organization for Septuagint and Cognate Studies and the SBLPS.* Edited by Robert A. Kraft. Missoula: Scholars Press, 1972. Pages 136-154.

Index

Abraham, 12, 21, 62, 85-89, 95, 101
altar, 2, 9, 46, 66
annihilation, iv, 9, 29, 61, 63, 96
anointed, 20-21, 29, 38, 64, 91
Antiochus IV Epiphanes, 45-46, 80-81
blessing, 8, 20-21, 45, 81, 83
bribes, 31
Charlesworth, James, v
chastise, 8, 17, 20, 62
Christians, iii, v-vi, 94, 96-97, 99, 101
corruption, 5, 10, 15, 17, 31, 48, 65
covenant, 12, 18, 45, 60-62, 81-82, 85-101
crown, 3, 10

cultic, 24-25, 39, 41-43, 45, 48-49, 51-53, 56-61, 65-70, 74, 76-78, 80-84, 88, 90, 92, 94-95, 100
David, 18-19, 94
destruction, 5, 11, 15-16, 19, 24-26, 34, 37-40, 42, 61-65, 68-69, 81-83, 90, 92-93, 96, 100
diadem, 3
De Jonge, Marinus, iii, v
Dunn, James, 96-98
earth, 1-3, 6-7, 9-11, 16, 18-20, 28-29, 35, 63-64
Egypt, 3, 51-52, 72, 74-75, 79
eternal damnation, 3
eternity, 4-5, 9, 11-18, 21, 63, 77, 82, 88
Exile, 23-25, 38-39, 41-45, 49, 51, 60-65, 68-72, 91-92, 95
extermination, iv
fear, viii, 3-4, 6, 15-16, 20-22, 62-63
feet, 8, 10, 62, 98
first-born, 15, 21
Gentiles, 3, 10, 12, 18-20, 25, 40, 47, 60, 62-63, 68-69, 91, 97
glory, 1-3, 8, 13, 18, 20, 26, 29, 38, 77-78, 80, 82-83
Gospel of John, 97-98
Greek, viii, 43

Index

Hasmoneans, viii, 50-51, 53-54, 57-58, 79-80, 83, 85, 94, 100
Hellenistic, viii, 44, 46-48, 53
High Priest, 43-44, 46-50, 52-54, 56, 73, 81, 83-84, 94
holy, 4-5, 8-16, 19-20, 39, 60, 62, 65-66, 70, 77-78, 81
Horbury, William, iii, v
ignorance, iii-iv, 14, 21, 33
ingathering, 13, 23, 42, 51, 70-72, 74-77, 80
Israel, iv, 3, 5, 8-14, 17-18, 20-21, 23, 25-26, 35, 39-40, 43-44, 47, 50-51, 54, 57, 61-62, 64-65, 70, 74-75, 77-78, 81-83, 87, 89-91
Jerusalem, iv, vii-viii, 2, 9-10, 13, 18-20, 23-26, 37-39, 41-54, 56-61, 63-82, 84-85, 92-96, 100-101
Jews, iii-vii, 23-26, 39-40, 42-43, 45-47, 51-52, 54-55, 57-58, 60, 61-66, 69-72, 74-78, 81-83, 87-88, 91-97, 99-101
judge, 3, 6, 9-11, 19-20, 25, 31, 68
justice, 19, 64
justify, 2
kill, 26, 34, 46, 55, 88, 93, 101

king, 3, 8, 18-21, 26, 29-30, 32, 34, 38, 64-65, 74, 81, 89-91, 94
laity, 53-55, 58
Leontopolis, 51-53, 73, 79
lies, 13
life, vi, viii, 4-6, 11, 15, 18, 40, 54, 76
Maccabean, 23, 43, 46-47, 49, 51, 79, 85
military, 36, 52, 55, 90
Mosaic Law, 54
name, 7-10, 12-13, 16, 18, 37, 43-44, 46, 65, 82-83, 86
Pharisees, vii, 53-56, 58
priests, vii-viii, 25, 38, 43, 48-51, 53, 57, 73, 77-81, 84
Presbyterian, 46
Qurman, 51-53, 79
religion, iv, vi-vii, 30-33, 35, 37, 42, 48-49, 55
Romans, 55, 96, 99
sacrifice, vi-vii, 10, 25, 27-28, 34-35, 39, 42, 66-68, 71, 77-78, 80, 100
Sadducees, 55-58
Sanders, E. P., 94-98
sectarian, 41
sects, 23
sexual, 66-67, 90
sinners, 1-2, 4-5, 12, 14-17, 19-20
Syria, 45

110

Index

Teacher of Righteousness, 52

temple, vi-viii, 8, 23-26, 29, 33, 37-64, 66-70, 72-73, 76-82, 84-85, 92-96, 99-101

transgression, 2, 5-6, 9, 13, 19, 65-68, 70

victory, 43, 46, 49, 64, 83

Wicked Priest, 52

Zadokites, viii, 48, 51-53, 58, 73, 80, 84-85, 94, 100

Zealots, 55, 58

About the Author

Professor Heerak Christian Kim is Adjunct Professor of Biblical Studies at Asia Evangelical College and Seminary in Bangalore, India. Professor Kim is an eminent professor of Jewish Studies, who has been trained by leading experts in Jewish Studies around the world – at Harvard University, Brown University, Cambridge University in Great Britain, Heidelberg University in Germany, the Hebrew University of Jerusalem in Israel, Fuller Theological Seminary, UCLA, and the University of Pennsylvania. Professor Kim held the prestigious Lady Davis Fellowship from 1996 to 1997. As a Lady Davis Fellow in the State of Israel, Professor Kim investigated the concept of Jewish individual identity and group identity. The interest in Jewish identity began in 1993, when Professor Kim was a Visiting Research Fellow at the Hebrew University of Jerusalem, while being a Ph.D. student in the History Department of UCLA. During that research year, Professor Kim investigated Jewish individual and group identity in the Thanksgiving Psalms (1QH and 4QH) from Qumran with Professor Daniel Schwartz, the Chairman of the Jewish History Department at the Hebrew University of Jerusalem. Professor Kim's interest in Jewish individual and group identity expanded in research scope when he was chosen as one of ten Raoul Wallenberg Scholars from the United States to the State of Israel from 1995 to 1996. As a Raoul Wallenberg Scholar, Prof. Kim conducted research into understanding Jewish identity through linguistic studies with the resident Hebrew linguist, Professor Avi Hurvitz of the Department of Hebrew and Aramaic Languages at the Hebrew University of Jerusalem.

Professor Avi Hurvitz is the global expert for synchronic and diachronic study of the Hebrew language. Professor Kim continues to be very active in academia, delivering academic papers around the world. Most recently, Professor Kim was invited to give a lecture on the Zadokites at the Seminar for the Use of the Old Testament in the New Testament in Great Britain (March 2008). Also, Professor Kim delivered a very important academic paper on the Zadokites and the Psalms of Solomon at the XIXth Congress of the International Organization for the Study of the Old Testament (IOSOT) in Ljubljana, Slovenia (July 2007). As a global expert on the Psalms of Solomon, Professor Kim is the author of the important academic monograph, *The Jerusalem Tradition in the Late Second Temple Period: Diachronic and Synchronic Developments Surrounding Psalms of Solomon 11* (University Press of America, 2006).

www.ingramcontent.com/pod-product-compliance
Lightning Source LLC
Chambersburg PA
CBHW021913180426
43198CB00034B/368